THE TEACHER'S PET
Time-Savers for All Reasons and Seasons

Written by Linda Schwartz
Illustrated by Beverly Armstrong
Edited by Sherri Butterfield

The Learning Works

Copyright © 1983
THE LEARNING WORKS, INC.
Santa Barbara, CA 93160
All rights reserved.
Printed in the United States of America.

Introduction

The Teacher's Pet is a time-saving collection of ready-to-use

- activities
- announcements
- awards
- birthday notes
- bookmarks
- borders
- calendars
- charts
- clip art
- contracts
- creative writing topics
- facts
- forms
- games
- get-well notes
- graphs
- holiday suggestions
- independent study ideas
- invitations
- letters
- lists
- memos
- miscellaneous information
- name tags
- patterns
- rules
- tables
- worksheets

Compiled by a former classroom teacher, these materials cover all major subject areas, including reading, language arts, math, social studies, and science, and are as up-to-date as computers. Many of them are all-purpose or open-ended and can be adapted easily to any event, occasion, or season. They have been selected for you, for your students, and for the aides, parents, substitutes, and others who work with you in educating children.

The pages in this book will help you get organized, get acquainted with your students, make assignments, keep track of student progress, give encouragement, recognize achievement, fill empty hours on rainy days, and communicate effectively with aides, substitute teachers, and parents—even when there isn't time! These pages will give students ideas for research projects and creative writing topics. They will help students explore word origins and meanings, increase their vocabularies, practice math skills, keep track of assignments, make contracts governing work and behavior, budget time, plan projects, organize reports, and evaluate results.

But teaching and learning should not be all forms and facts. There's got to be some fun. Border patterns will help you decorate bulletin boards and walls. Clip art cutouts will make it easy for you to add a touch of whimsy to the tests and worksheets you create and to the announcements and letters you send home.

The Teacher's Pet doesn't teach. Only you can do that. But its pages are packed with possibilities—ways to make teaching easier for you and learning more fun for your students. It's all of the many facts, forms, and ideas you need in one single, convenient package.

Contents

Forms and Notes **7-42**

Forms for Teachers **8-12**
Birthday Scoops 8
All-Purpose Chart 9
Any Month Calendar 10
Things to Do 11
Handy Home Information 12

Forms for Parents **13-19**
A Call for Supplies 13
Portrait of Our Day 14
Supply Checklist 15
All About Assignments 16
Assignments 17
Help Wanted 18
Class Newsletter 19

Forms for Students **20-27**
Reading Worksheet 20
Home Reading Record 21
Homework Assignments 22
Make-up Memo 23
Student Contract 24
Behavior Contract 25
Field Trip Frame-ups 26
Test-Taking Tips 27

Forms for Substitutes and Aides **28-34**
Helpful Hints for My Substitute 28
Lesson Plans for My Substitute 29
Class List for My Substitute 30
Aide Assignment Sheet: Working with Students 31
Aide Assignment Sheet: Clerical Duties 32
Activity Evaluation Sheet for Aides 33

Aide Awards 34

Name Tags and Notes **35-42**
Name Tags 35
General Notes 36
Reminders 37
Announcements 38
Invitations 39
Thank-You Notes 40
Get-Well Notes 41
Happy Birthday Notes 42

Getting to Know You **43-50**
How I See Me 44
Who Are You? 45
My All-Time Favorites 46
Spare-Time Checklist 47
The I-N-G Me 48
Personality Cubes 49
My Crystal Ball 50

Language Arts **51-96**
Rules for Dividing Words into Syllables 52
Rules for Accenting Syllables 53
Great Ideas for Using the Synonym, Antonym,
and Homonym Lists on Pages 59-62 54
Roots 55
Prefixes 56-57
Suffixes 58
Synonyms 59
Antonyms 60
Hundreds of Homonyms 61-62
Parts of Speech 63

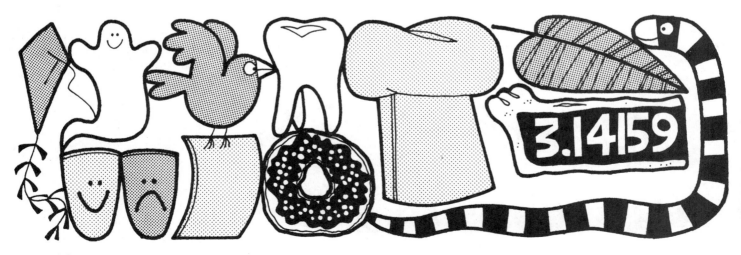

Contents
(continued)

Rules of Punctuation. 64-65
Rules for Forming Plurals 66
Great Ideas for Using Hyphenated Words
and Compound Words on Pages 68-70 67
Hyphenated Happenings 68
Compound Capers 69-70
Contraction Critter 71
Word of the Week 72-75
Great Ideas for Using the Creative
Writing Topics Listed on Pages 77-81 76
Creative Writing Topics
    Sports 77
    Mystery 78
    Animal Stories 79
    Just for Fun 80
    General 81
Book Report Brainstorms 82
Fiction Facts 83
Read All About It Press 84
Got the Plot? 85
The Dewey Decimal System of Classification 86
The Parts of a Book 87
My Vocabulary List 88
Bookmarks 89
Pickled Plurals 90
Create a Word 91
Spelling Riddle 92
What Would You Do With . . . ? 93
Hat Happenings 94
Cross Country Cryptogram 95
The Case of the Missing Masterpiece 96

Math **97-108**
Addition Table 98
Blank Addition Table 99
Multiplication Table 100
Blank Multiplication Table 101
The Sum's the Same 102
How Strong Is Your Addition? 103
Find Five Subtraction Quiz 104
Multiplication Quiz 105
Doughnuts Division 106
Graphs Galore 107
More Graphs Galore 108

Social Studies **109-124**
Ideas for Social Studies Projects 110
Fifty Nifty Topics for Social Studies Research 111
Map of the United States 112
Map Quiz 113
Abbreviations for State Names 114
Map of Canada 115
Map of the World 116
Where in the World Are You From? 117
My Family Tree 118
People Posters 119
Research a Country 120
Stamps for Research a Country 121-122
Latitude and Longitude 123
Time Zones 124

Science **125-144**
Ideas for Science Projects 126

Contents
(continued)

Sixty Sensational Science Topics 127
Great Ideas for Using the Lists
on Pages 132-136 128-129
Category Game 130
Category Game Sheet 131
Flower Power 132
Treasury of Trees 133
Fish Frenzy 134
Bunches of Birds 135
Mammal Mania 136
Science Project Worksheet 137
Computer Talk 138-142
Hobbies and Occupations 143-144

Awards **145-156**

All-Purpose Awards 146
Effort and Improvement Awards 147
Reading and Book Reporting Awards 148
Spelling and Handwriting Awards 149
Other Language Arts Awards 150
Addition and Subtraction Awards 151
Multiplication and Division Awards 152
Other Math Awards 153
Social Studies Awards 154
Science Awards 155
Art and Sports Awards 156

Holiday Happenings **157-191**

Multipurpose Worksheets **158-169**
Back-to-School Apples 158
Floating Ghosts 159
Turkey Trot 160

Pick a Package 161
Happy New Year Hats 162
Have a Heart 163
Lucky Shamrocks 164
Funny Bunnies 165
Kite Flight 166
Summer Suns 167
Flying Flags 168
Dandy Daisies 169

Clip Art **170-181**
Clip Art 170
Happy Holidays 171-173
Ways to Go 174
Space Race 175
Sports Shorts 176
Discoveries and Inventions 177
Animal Antics 178
On Stage 179
Characters and Careers 180-181

Borders **182-191**
Borders 182
Acorns and Leaves 183
Pumpkins and Cats 184
Ships and Turkeys 185
Mice and Bells 186
Snowmen and Mittens 187
Hats and Hearts 188
Shamrocks and Tulips 189
Umbrellas and Bunnies 190
Daisies and Suns 191

Answer Key **192**

Forms and Notes

Birthday Scoops

Write each child's name, birthdate,
and age in the appropriate place.
Then keep this sheet for reference.

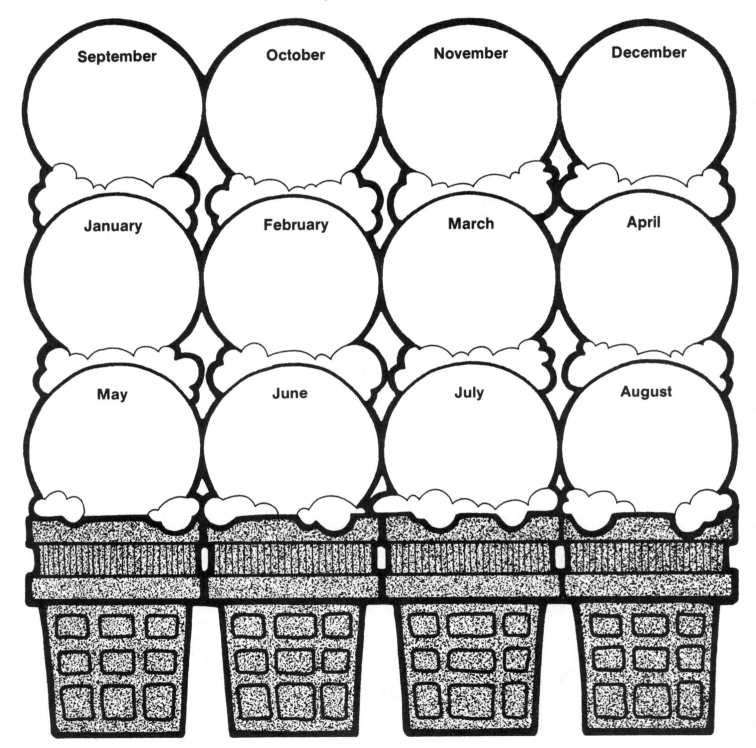

All-Purpose Chart

Any Month Calendar

SUNDAY	MONDAY	TUESDAY	WEDNESDAY	THURSDAY	FRIDAY	SATURDAY

Date _____

Things to Do

Things to Do

Appointments to Keep

Person	Time	Place

Phone Calls to Make

Person	Number

Handy Home Information

Name	Address	Telephone

A Call for Supplies

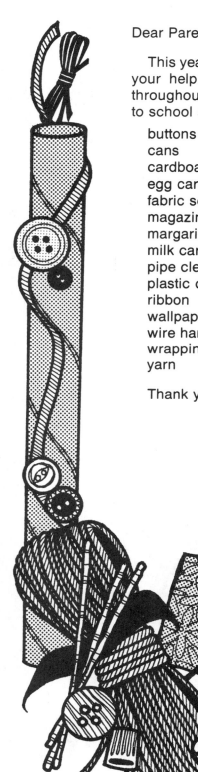

Dear Parents,

This year our class will be involved in many exciting projects. We need your help in gathering the supplies and materials that will be used throughout the school year in our crafts center. Please help us by sending to school any of the following materials that you would like to donate:

buttons
cans
cardboard tubes
egg cartons
fabric scraps
magazines
margarine tubs
milk cartons
pipe cleaners
plastic containers of various sizes
ribbon
wallpaper scraps
wire hangers
wrapping paper
yarn

Thank you for your help.

Sincerely,

_____

Portrait of Our Day

Dear Parents,

We hope you will come to see our classroom. Here's a copy of our daily schedule to help you plan your visit.

Sincerely,

_____

Time	Subject

School begins at _____

Morning recess _____

Lunchtime _____

Afternoon recess _____

Dismissal _____

Special Programs

Art _____

Music _____

Physical Education _____

Others _____

_____

Supply Checklist

Dear Parents,

Your child needs the supplies checked below for projects we will be doing in class.

- ☐ box for supplies
- ☐ pen
- ☐ pencils
- ☐ erasers
- ☐ ruler
- ☐ paste or white school glue
- ☐ crayons
- ☐ felt-tipped marking pens in assorted colors
- ☐ compass
- ☐ protractor
- ☐ folder(s)
- ☐ three-ring binder
- ☐ lined notebook paper
- ☐ unlined notebook paper
- ☐ graph paper
- ☐ construction paper in the following colors:

_____   _____

_____   _____

_____   _____

- ☐ hole punch
- ☐ old shirt to be used as an artist's smock

Please put your child's name on each item. A reminder will be sent home when our classroom supplies need to be replenished.

Thank you for your cooperation.

Sincerely,

_____

All About Assignments

Dear Parents,

Communication between home and school is vital to your child's success in the classroom.

To keep you informed and aware of what we are doing, I plan to send home a folder with papers and tests your child has completed in all areas of the curriculum every _____ .

Please take the time to review and discuss these papers with your child. Then date and initial the form on your child's folder, keep the papers (unless otherwise noted), and have your child return the empty folder to me within two days.

Your cooperation is greatly appreciated.

Sincerely,

_____

Assignments

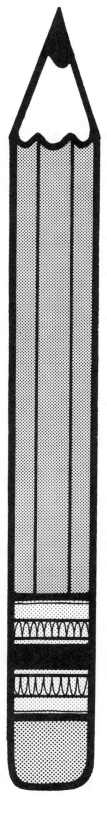

Dear Parents,

Inside this folder/envelope are _____
papers for the week. Please take time to review and discuss them with your
child. Then date and initial this form and have your child return the empty
folder to me by _____ of each week.

Date	Parent's Signature	Parent's Comments

Help Wanted

Dear Parents,

We will be involved in a variety of projects during this school year and would appreciate your help. Please take time to fill out the attached form and have your child return it to me as soon as possible.

Sincerely,

_____

Name _____

Address _____

Phone _____

1. I am willing to help in the following areas:

   ☐ room mother   ☐ dancing
   ☐ assistant room mother   ☐ arts and crafts
   ☐ phone committee   ☐ physical education
   ☐ sewing   ☐ field trips
   ☐ cooking   ☐ _____
   ☐ carpentry   ☐ _____
   ☐ drama   ☐ _____
   ☐ music   ☐ _____

2. I would enjoy

   ☐ working with individual   ☐ making games
     students   ☐ typing
   ☐ working with small groups   ☐ performing other clerical tasks
   ☐ duplicating worksheets   ☐ _____
   ☐ grading papers   ☐ _____
   ☐ preparing learning centers   ☐ _____

3. I have the following special interest, talent, hobby, or occupation I would be willing to share with the class:

   _____

4. The best time for me to help in the class is on
   ☐ Monday ☐ Tuesday ☐ Wednesday ☐ Thursday ☐ Friday

   at _____ o'clock.

CLASS NEWSLETTER

DATE: ISSUE NUMBER:

FOCUS ON . . .

CLASSROOM ORIGINALS

READING

MATH

SCIENCE

SOCIAL STUDIES

OTHER

SUGGESTIONS FOR PARENTS

CALENDAR

Reading Worksheet
for the
Week of _____

Name _____ **Reading Group** _____

Read

Seat Work

Learning Center

****
_____
_____
_____
_____
****

Schedule

Monday	Tuesday	Wednesday	Thursday	Friday

Special Assignments _____

_____

Conference _____

Home Reading Record

Name _____

Date Started	Title	Author	Number of Pages	Date Finished

Homework Assignments
for the week of _____

READING

Monday _____

Tuesday _____

Wednesday _____

Thursday _____

Friday _____

MATH

Monday _____

Tuesday _____

Wednesday _____

Thursday _____

Friday _____

SCIENCE OR SOCIAL STUDIES

Monday _____

Tuesday _____

Wednesday _____

Thursday _____

Friday _____

SPELLING

Mon. _____

Tues. _____

Wed. _____

Thurs. _____

Fri. _____

OTHER

Mon. _____

Tues. _____

Wed. _____

Thurs. _____

Fri. _____

Make-up Memo

To: _____

From: _____ Date: _____

Welcome back! While you were absent on _____ ,
you missed the following classwork assignments:

Reading _____
_____
_____

Math _____
_____
_____

Spelling _____
_____
_____

Social Studies _____
_____
_____

Science _____
_____
_____

Other _____
_____
_____

Please complete these assignments and turn them in to me on or before _____ .

Student Contract

1. I plan to do research on the following topic: _____

   _____

2. Some of the subtopics I plan to cover are

   _____   _____

   _____   _____

3. The purpose of my project is to _____

   _____ .

4. Several things I hope to find out are _____

   _____

   _____ .

5. In doing my project, I will use the following resources (check all that apply):

   ☐ atlas   ☐ other books   ☐ pamphlets
   ☐ dictionary   ☐ films/filmstrips   ☐ pictures
   ☐ encyclopedia   ☐ interviews   ☐ records
   ☐ textbooks   ☐ magazines   ☐ tapes
   ☐ Who's Who   ☐ maps   ☐ experimentation
   ☐ world almanac   ☐ newspapers   ☐ observation

   ☐ other: _____

6. My final presentation will take the form of a/an

   ☐ chart   ☐ graph   ☐ poster
   ☐ diorama   ☐ map   ☐ scrapbook
   ☐ film/filmstrip   ☐ model   ☐ tape recording
   ☐ game   ☐ oral report   ☐ written report

   ☐ other: _____

7. I plan to complete my project on or before _____ .

8. I will evaluate my project in the following manner: _____

   _____

   _____   _____
   (student's signature)   (teacher's signature)

   _____   _____
   (date)   (date)

Behavior Contract

I, _____ , do hereby

declare on this _____ day of _____

in the year _____ , that I will

- ☐ arrive at school on time.
- ☐ listen better in class.
- ☐ have a sharp pencil, clean paper, or other materials ready when needed.
- ☐ put forth more effort.
- ☐ be neater in my work.
- ☐ complete all assignments to the best of my ability.
- ☐ turn in each assignment on time.
- ☐ improve my weekly spelling test score by _____ points.
- ☐ be more considerate of others.
- ☐ get along better with my classmates.
- ☐ make better use of my study time.
- ☐ make better use of my free time.
- ☐ keep the top of my desk neat.
- ☐ keep the inside of my desk neat.
- ☐ help keep the room clean by _____
- ☐ _____

_____
Signature

_____
Witness

Name _____

Field Trip Frame-ups

Date _____

Place I Visited _____

_____

_____

_____

Fascinating Things I Saw

_____

_____

_____

_____

Some Things I Learned

_____

_____

_____

_____

_____

New Words I Know

_____

_____

_____

_____

Picture I Drew to Remind Me of the Trip

Test-Taking Tips

General

1. Be prepared to do your best. Review the material, get plenty of sleep on the night before the test, and eat a good breakfast on the morning of the test.
2. Bring all needed materials, such as pencils, erasers, and scratch paper, to the test.
3. Pay attention to the oral instructions.
4. Read the written instructions carefully.
5. Ask questions if you do not understand any of the instructions.
6. Know how much time you have, and use it wisely.
7. If you finish a section and have extra time, spend it looking back over your work and checking your answers.

Standardized Tests

1. Don't sharpen your pencil to a fine point. The answer slots, circles, or boxes can be filled in more easily with a blunt pencil.
2. Speed is essential, so answer the questions you feel confident about first. Then go back to the questions that will take more of your time.
3. Answer every question. Most standardized tests are scored on the basis of the total number of correct answers, so it's a good idea to make a guess when you are not sure of an answer.
4. Before you mark the answer sheet, check the question number against the answer number so that you won't mark a right answer in the wrong place.

True-and-False Tests

1. Read each statement carefully. Sometimes a single word can trick you into giving the wrong answer.
2. When you see such words as **never**, **all**, and **always**, the statement is usually false.
3. In two-part statements, read each part carefully. If one part is true but the other part is false, the entire statement is false.

Essay Tests

1. Read each question and be sure that you understand what is being asked.
2. Underline important clue words and phrases to help you focus your answer. Look for such words as **list**, **describe**, and **compare**.
3. Plan your answer before you begin to write.
4. If there is more than one question, decide how to divide your time. Allot more time to the harder questions or to the questions that are worth more points.
5. Write clearly and concisely.
6. Back up your definitions and explanations with specific examples.
7. If you are uncertain about the answer to a question, write something. You may know more than you think you do.
8. Proofread your essays to be certain that the spelling, punctuation, and grammar are correct; that you have said what you intended to say; and that you have not left out important information or failed to make an essential point.

🍀 Helpful Hints 🍀
For My Substitute

1. A teacher who can help you is _____ in room _____.

2. Dependable students who can help you are _____
   _____.

3. Classroom aides or volunteers who are scheduled to come in today are

Name	Time	Assignment
_____	_____	_____
_____	_____	_____
_____	_____	_____

4. You will find the following essential items in the places indicated.

   Grade book _____

   Lesson plans _____

   Seating chart _____

   Teacher's manuals _____

5. My duty today is _____
      (job)
   at _____ at _____.
      (place)   (time)

6. My usual roll-call procedure is _____
   _____.

7. The following students will be leaving the classroom during the day to attend special classes or to keep scheduled appointments:

Name	Time	Class/Reason	Room
_____	_____	_____	_____
_____	_____	_____	_____
_____	_____	_____	_____
_____	_____	_____	_____

8. The students on medication are _____
   _____.

9. Emergency procedures are as follows: _____
   _____
   _____

Lesson Plans
For My Substitute

Daily Schedule

Class Begins _____
Morning Recess _____
Lunch _____
Afternoon Recess _____
Dismissal _____

Date _____

Time	Subject	Description

Class List
For My Substitute

Girls

Boys

Aide Assignment Sheet
Working with Students

Name _____   **Date** _____

Activity	Student(s) Involved	Comments
☐ Listen to oral reading		
☐ Record dictation		
☐ Review flash cards		
☐ Assist with the following learning center activity:		
☐ Assist the following reading, math, writing, or spelling group:		
☐ Other		

❀✳ Aide Assignment Sheet ✳❀
Clerical Duties

Name _____   Date _____

Activity	Special Instructions	Needed By
☐ Type ditto masters	☐ of pages _____ in _____ ☐ of the attached sheets	
☐ Make a thermofax master	☐ of pages _____ in _____ ☐ of the attached sheets	
☐ Alphabetize		
☐ File		
☐ Run copies of _____	Number of copies needed _____ Print ☐ on one side ☐ on two sides	
☐ Grade the attached papers		
☐ Make the described game or activity		
☐ Cut paper	Type of paper _____ Color(s) _____ Number of sheets _____ Dimensions _____	
☐ Design a calendar for the month of _____	Suggested picture or theme _____ _____ _____	
☐ Design a bulletin board	Subject _____ Theme _____ Purpose _____	

Activity Evaluation Sheet
For Aides

Name _____ **Date** _____

Assignment _____

To help me evaluate the effectiveness of the activity you supervised, please fill out this sheet and return it to me.

1. I felt that the activity was
   ☐ very effective
   ☐ satisfactory
   ☐ ineffective because _____
   _____
   _____.

2. The following students had difficulty with the activity:
   _____
   _____

3. The behavior of the following students was a problem:
   _____
   _____

4. If the activity is done again, I would suggest that the following changes be made:
   _____
   _____
   _____

5. Additional comments or suggestions: _____
   _____
   _____
   _____

Aide Awards

Name Tags

These all-purpose name tags are ideal for use by substitutes, visitors, and guest speakers and for use on field trips, at open house, and on many other occasions.

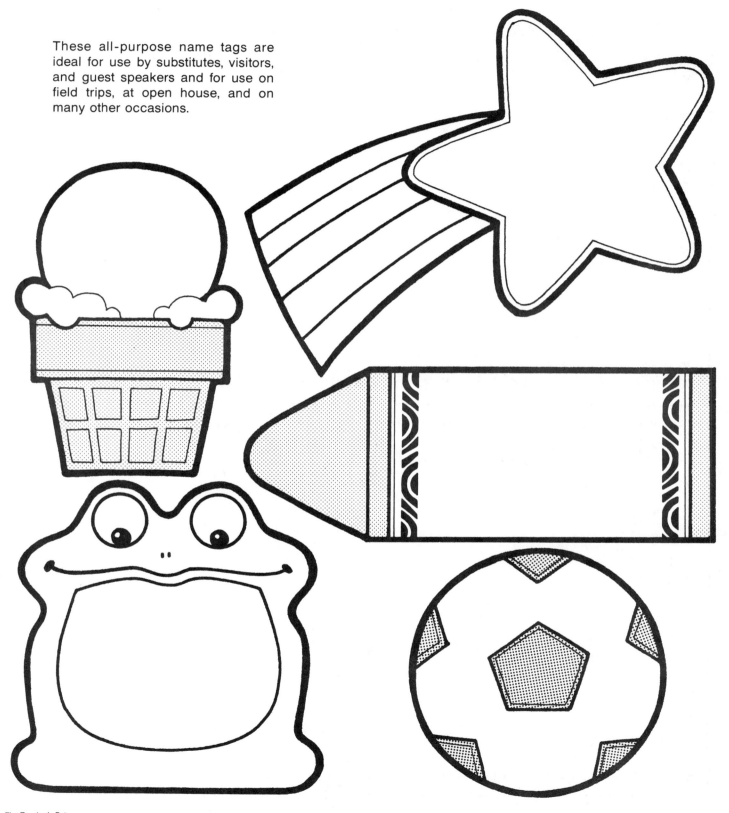

General Notes

CLASSROOM CALENDAR

TEACHER TALK

FROM THE DESK OF

Reminders

Announcements

Invitations

Thank-You Notes

Get-Well Notes

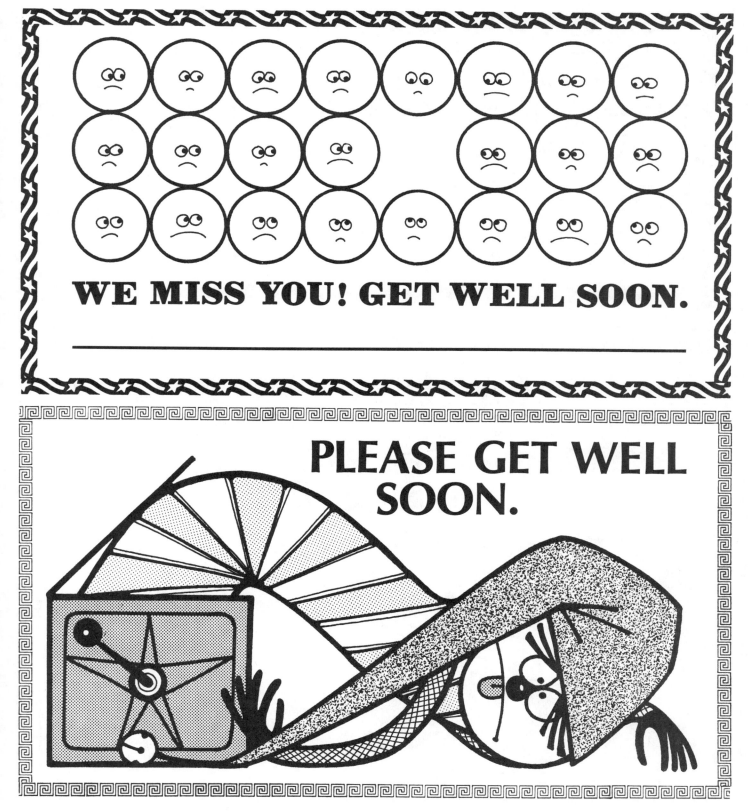

Happy Birthday Notes

Getting to Know You

How I See Me

Here is a picture of how I see myself on _____ .

(today's date)

Name _____

Try this activity again later in the school year. Compare your two pictures, and see how you've changed.

Who Are You?

My name is _____

1. Five things I like are

    a. _____

    b. _____

    c. _____

    d. _____

    e. _____

2. Five things I dislike are

    a. _____

    b. _____

    c. _____

    d. _____

    e. _____

3. My three most important strengths are

    a. _____

    b. _____

    c. _____

4. The three areas I want to improve are

    a. _____

    b. _____

    c. _____

5. I like to collect _____.

6. Outside school I take lessons in _____.

7. I think it would be fun to learn more about _____

Name _____

My All-Time Favorites

actor/actress	_____
age	_____
animal	_____
athlete	_____
beverage	_____
book	_____
color	_____
day of the week	_____
food	_____
game	_____
hobby	_____
holiday	_____
magazine	_____
movie	_____
number	_____
person	_____
place to visit	_____
record or tape	_____
restaurant	_____
song	_____
sport	_____
subject in school	_____
television show	_____
thing to wear	_____

Name _____

Spare-Time Checklist

In my spare time I like to

☐ camp
☐ climb trees
☐ do puzzles
☐ draw and color
☐ finger-paint
☐ fly kites
☐ go to movies
☐ jump rope

☐ listen to music
☐ make jewelry
☐ make models
☐ paint
☐ play a musical instrument
☐ read
☐ ride a bike
☐ ride a horse

☐ roller skate
☐ sew
☐ ski
☐ surf
☐ swim
☐ visit friends
☐ watch television
☐ _____

I collect

☐ cards
☐ coins
☐ dolls
☐ models
☐ _____

☐ rocks
☐ shells
☐ stamps

I enjoy playing

☐ baseball
☐ basketball
☐ cards
☐ checkers
☐ chess
☐ dominoes
☐ football
☐ _____
☐ _____

☐ hockey
☐ marbles
☐ ping-pong
☐ shuffleboard
☐ soccer
☐ tennis
☐ video games

I like to read

☐ animal stories
☐ biographies
☐ comic books
☐ detective stories
☐ fables
☐ fairy tales
☐ fantasy
☐ history
☐ mysteries
☐ poetry
☐ science fiction
☐ sports stories
☐ tales of horror and suspense
☐ tall tales
☐ westerns
☐ _____
☐ _____

Name _____

The I-N-G Me

Here are three words ending in i-n-g
that I can use to describe me.

1. _____

2. _____

3. _____

laughing   **eating**   **singing**

In the boxes below are pictures of me doing my three i-n-g words.

Name _____

Personality Cubes

What You Need

empty cardboard box
scissors
white glue
magazines (for pictures and words)
felt-tipped marking pens in assorted colors
crayons
paint
paintbrush
colored paper (butcher, shelf, wall, or wrapping paper)

What You Do

1. Bring an empty cardboard box to class.

2. Cover the box with colored paper.

3. Decorate the box with pictures and words cut from magazines, or draw sketches and write words that tell about you. Use one side of the box for each of the following topics:
   - likes
   - dislikes
   - family and friends
   - hobbies and interests
   - strengths and weaknesses
   - plans for the future

My Crystal Ball

HERE'S A PICTURE OF SOMETHING I'LL BE DOING THIS SUMMER.

HERE'S A PICTURE OF A PLACE I'D LIKE TO VISIT SOMEDAY.

HERE'S A PICTURE OF THE JOB I'D LIKE TO HAVE.

Language Arts

Rules for Dividing Words into Syllables

1. A syllable is a group of letters sounded together.

2. Each syllable must have at least one vowel sound.

3. A word cannot have more syllables than vowel sounds.

4. Words pronounced as one syllable should not be divided.

   dive   helped   through

5. A word containing two consonants between two vowels (**vccv**) is divided between the two consonants.

   vc cv   **vc cv**   **vc cv**
   cor-rect   pret-ty   sis-ter

6. In a two-syllable word containing a single consonant between two vowels (**vcv**), the consonant usually begins the second syllable.

   v cv   **v cv**
   po-tion   to-day

7. In a word ending in **-le**, the consonant immediately preceding the **-le** usually begins the last syllable.

   can-dle   mar-ble   ta-ble

8. Compound words usually are divided between their word parts.

   down-stairs   rain-bow   sun-shine

9. In a word containing a prefix, the prefix usually forms a separate syllable.

   ex-plain   re-turn

10. In a word containing a suffix, the suffix usually forms a separate syllable.

    help-ful   kind-ness

Rules for Accenting Syllables

1. In a two-syllable word containing a double consonant, the first syllable is usually accented.

    hap′ py   rib′ bon

2. In a two-syllable word where the second syllable has two vowels, the second syllable is usually accented.

    con ceive′   de fraud′   pre mier′

3. In words ending in **-ion**, **-tion**, **-sion**, **-ial**, and **-cial**, the syllable preceding these endings is usually accented.

    dis cus′ sion   ex ten′ sion   of fi′ cial   po ten′ tial

4. In a word containing a prefix, the accent usually falls on or within the root word.

    com pose′   in doors′   re ply′

5. In a compound word, the accent usually falls on or within the first word.

    black′ board   court′ house   farm′ hand   surf′ board

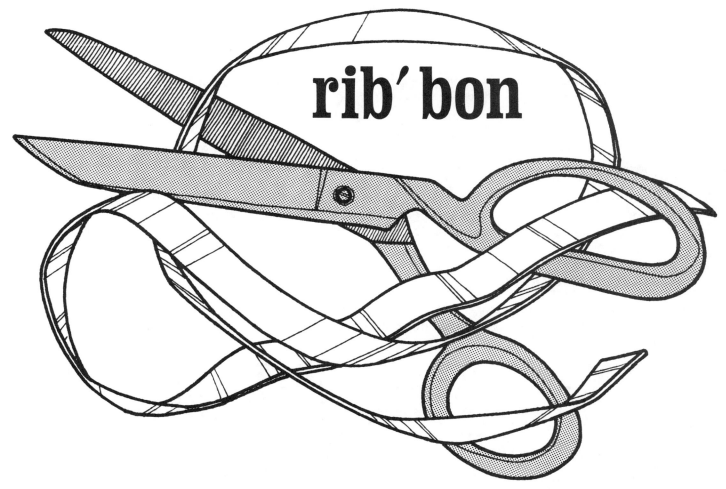

Great Ideas
For Using the Synonym, Antonym, and
Homonym Lists on Pages 59-62

Crossword Creations

Give each student a copy of one list of words. Have students create their own crossword puzzles using either synonyms, antonyms, or homonyms.

Homonym Hunt

Have each student write a story using twenty-five homonyms incorrectly. Tell students to exchange stories and circle all of the misused homonyms. Then have them write the correct spelling of each circled homonym.

Concentration

Select ten pairs of words from one of the lists. Write each word on an index card. Shuffle the cards and place them face down. In turn, players turn over two cards, trying to find a matched pair of synonyms, homonyms, or antonyms. If a pair is found, the player takes another turn. If the cards turned over are not a matched pair, they are turned face down in their original positions, and play continues clockwise. When all of the cards have been matched correctly, the player with the most pairs is the winner.

Two-in-Ten Sentences

Have students pick ten pairs of words from either the homonym or the antonym list and write ten sentences using one pair of words in each sentence.

Examples: The wind <u>blew</u> over the <u>blue</u> sea.
Multiplication is <u>simple</u>, but geometry is <u>complex.</u>

Homonym Dig

Have students work alone, in pairs, or in teams to compile lists of homonyms. Encourage them to use dictionaries. See who can reach one hundred first or who can list the most. Or suggest that everyone in the class work together to create an on-going list of homonyms and try to top three hundred!

Antonym Pantomime

Have each student pick a pair of antonyms and pantomime the words, one at a time, for other class members. Tell students to wait until both words have been pantomimed before beginning to guess the antonyms.

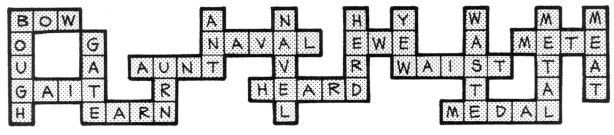

Roots

*act, *do, drive*
act
action
activate
active
actor
actual
exact
exactly
inactive
inactivity
react
transact

*circle, **cycle**, *ring, complete period, wheel*
bicycle
bicyclist
circle
circular
circulation
circus
cycle
cyclone
encyclopedia
motorcycle
recycle
tricycle
tricyclist
unicycle

*fact, **feat**, **fic**, *to make, act, deed, thing done*
defeat
fact
factory
feat
fiction
manufacture
nonfiction

*fer, *bring, bear, carry, put*
confer
conference
ferry
offer
prefer
preferable
preference
refer
reference
suffer
transfer
transferable

*jac, **ject**, *throw or cast*
dejected
eject
injection
interject
jaculate
project
projectionist
projectile
projector
reject
subject

*mob, **mot**, **mov**, *move, movable, moving*
automobile
demote
immobile
immovable
locomotive
mobile
mobilization
mobilize
motion
motionless
motive
motor
motorboat
motorcycle
movement
movie
promote
promoter
promotion

*pone, **pos(e)**, **posit**, *lay down, put, place*
compose
composer
depose
deposit
disposable
opposite
position
postpone
preposition
propose
purpose
suppose

*port, *carry*
airport
deport
export
import
portable
report
reporter
support
transport
transportation

*tain, **ten(d)**, *hold*
attend
attention
contain
container
detain
entertainer
extend
intend
pretend
tent

*vid, **vis**, **view**, *see*
interview
interviewer
invisible
preview
previewer
provide
review
supervisor
television
video
visible
vision
visit
visitor
visualize

Prefixes

*anti-, *against, opposite of*
antiaircraft
antidote
antifreeze

*bi-, *two, once in every two*
biannual
bicameral
bicentennial
bicycle
bicyclist
biweekly

*co-, col-, com-, con-, cor-, *with, together*
coauthor
coexist
collect
collection
collectors
combine
comfort
command
companion
company
compare
complete
completely
compose
composer
compound
conductor
conference
confess
conform
connect
contact
contain
container
contest
continue
contract
cooperate
copilot
correct

*de-, *opposite of, remove from, reduce or lower*
deceive
decide

decode
decrease
defeat
defect
defector
defend
defense
deflate
defrost
dejected
delight
delightful
demote
depend
deplane
deport
depose
deposit
describe
detain
detect
dethrone

*dis-, *not, reverse, opposite of, apart, away from*
disagree
disappear
disappoint
disapprove
disarm
disbelief
disclose
disconnect
discount
discover
discovery
disguise
disgusting
dishearten
dishonest
dishonor
disinfect
disinterested
dislike
dismiss
disobey
disorderly
displease
disposable
disrobe
dissatisfy

*ex-, *former, before, from, out of, beyond*
exact
exactly
excellent
except
excite
exciting
excuse
exit
explain
explore
export
exportation
extend
exterior

*il-, im-, in-, ir-, *not, without*
illegal
immobile
immovable
impolite
impossible
impure
inactive
inactivity
incorrect
inferior
invisible
irregular

*im-, in-, *in, into*
import
impose
imprint
imprison
improve
income
increase
indeed
indent
indoors
infect
infection
infield
inform
injection
inland
inside
inspect
inspector

instant
instead
intake
intend
invite

*inter-, *between, among, jointly, together*
interchange
interfere
interject
interlock
intermediate
intermission
international
interoffice
interregnum
interstate
interview
interviewer

*mis-, *wrong, wrongly, bad, badly*
misbehave
misconduct
misdirect
misfortune
mishandle
misjudge
mislay
mislead
misleading
misplace
misprint
misquote
misread
misspell
mistake
mistaken
mistreat
mistrust

*n-, non-, *not*
neither
never
none
nonsense
nonstop
nor

Prefixes
(continued)

✳per-, *through, throughout, thoroughly*
perceive
percent
perchance
perfect
perfection
perform
performed
perfume

✳post-, *after, later*
postdate
postgame
postpone

✳pre-, *before or at an earlier time, in front of*
prefer
preferable
preference
prefix
preform
pregame
prehistoric
premature
prepare
prepay
preposition
preschool
present
pretend
preview

✳pro-, *before, forward, for, in front of, in favor of*
produce
product
project
projection
projector
promise
promote
promoter
pronoun
propeller
propose
protect
provide

✳re-, *again, back*
react
rebound
rebuild
recall
receive
reconnect
record
recover
recycle
redirect
redo
refer
reference
refinish
reform
reject
rejoice
relock
remain
remember
remind
remote
remove
repair
repay
repeat
replay
report
reporter
reprint
retitle
retold
retrace
return
reunite
review

✳sub-, **sup-**, *under, not up to, part of a whole*
subdivide
subject
submarine
submerge
subsoil
substitute
subtitle
subtract
subtraction

subway
superior
support
suppose
supposedly

✳super-, *over, above, higher in rank, greater in quality or amount*
superbowl
superheat
superhighway
superior
superman
supermarket
superstar
supervisor

✳trans-, *across, beyond, through, so as to change*
transact
transatlantic
transfer
transferable
transform
transistor
transoceanic
transplant
transport
transportation

✳tri-, *three, once in every three, three times during every*
triangle
tricolor
tricycle
tricyclist
trimonthly
trio
triple
triplets
tripod
triweekly

✳un-, *not*
unable
unarmed
unbeaten
unbutton
unclean
uncomfortable
uncooked
uncovered
undefeated
undiscovered
undivided
undone
undress
uneducated
unfair
unfinished
unfold
unfriendly
unhappy
unhurt
unimportant
unkind
unless
unlike
unlock
unlucky
unquestionable
unreal
unseeing
untrue
unwilling

✳uni-, *one*
unicameral
unicorn
unicycle
uniform
unilateral

Suffixes

✻-able, -ible, *able to, capable or worthy of, tending or likely to*
abominable
acceptable
agreeable
changeable
comfortable
disposable
drinkable
enjoyable
likable
lovable
movable
portable
possible
preferable
questionable
reproducible
teachable
transferable
understandable
visible

✻-ar, -er, -or, -r, *one who or something that*
actor
adventurer
author
banker
beggar
bookkeeper
buyer
chopper
collector
composer
conductor
container
dancer
defector
director
governor
helper
inspector
interviewer
liar
officer
overseer
porter
projector
prospector
protector

recorder
reporter
robber
ruler
sailor
supervisor
surfer
teacher
visitor
whistler
writer

✻-en, -n, *made of, of or belonging to, cause to be*
darken
golden
leaden
silken
weaken
wooden
woolen

✻-ful, *full of, characterized by*
beautiful
careful
delightful
faithful
fearful
grateful
hopeful
meaningful
plentiful
powerful
shameful
successful
thankful
wonderful

✻-ion, -tion, *act or process of, state or condition, result of*
action
addition
attention

circulation
collection
completion
exportation
infection
injection
intermission
mobilization
motion
pollution
position
preposition
projection
subtraction
television
transportation
vision

✻-ist, *one who makes, produces, or performs; one who is skilled in*
artist
balloonist
bicyclist
dentist
druggist
parachutist
projectionist
psychologist
scientist

✻-less, *without, lacking in*
ageless
breathless
careless
countless
endless
fearless
motionless
powerless
priceless
sleepless
spotless
useless

✻-ly, *in a certain manner, like, occurring every, in a certain place*
accidentally
badly
bravely
brotherly
closely
completely
correctly
deeply
doubly
exactly
friendly
highly
kindly
lonely
quarterly
really
reportedly
suddenly
supposedly
truly
yearly

✻-ness, *manner, state of being, quality, amount, degree*
carelessness
darkness
fairness
happiness
likeness

✻-y, *characterized by, full of, tending or inclined to*
creepy
curly
dirty
dusty
grassy
hairy
icy
lucky
noisy
oily
smoky
snowy

Synonyms

abrupt–sudden
adjust–fix
aid–assist
alone–solitary
anger–rage
answer–reply
arouse–awaken
beg–plead
blank–empty
brave–fearless
buy–purchase
calm–serene
caution–warn
choice–option
clear–plain
close–near
coarse–rough
coy–shy
danger–peril
decline–refuse
decrease–lessen
dense–thick
desire–want
detach–separate
disappear–vanish
divulge–disclose
dubious–doubtful
easy–simple
elect–choose
empty–vacant
enemy–rival
enormous–gigantic
extraordinary–unusual

false–untrue
fast–quick
fear–fright
fierce–ferocious
forgive–excuse
genuine–real
gleam–shine
govern–rule
grief–sorrow
happen–occur
hardy–strong
honest–sincere
hurry–rush
identical–alike
ill–sick
imitate–copy
inquire–ask
late–tardy
leave–depart
liberty–freedom
limp–slack
marvelous–wonderful
meek–mild
mend–repair
merit–worth
misty–foggy
mix–blend
modern–recent
moist–damp
necessary–essential
need–require
nimble–spry
normal–ordinary

obvious–apparent
odor–smell
often–frequently
opinion–view
oppose–resist
pain–ache
peculiar–odd
petty–trivial
piece–part
promise–pledge
quiver–shake
reasonable–fair
recall–remember
refuse–decline
reimburse–repay
sensible–wise
separate–disconnect
severe–harsh
shiver–shake
silly–foolish
small–tiny
task–job
teach–instruct
tease–taunt
tight–snug
timid–shy
tranquil–peaceful
useless–worthless
value–worth
verdict–judgment
whole–entire
worthy–honorable
zone–area

Antonyms

abate-increase
above-below
absent-present
accept-refuse
achieve-fail
active-passive
advance-retreat
alike-different
allow-forbid
always-never
ambitious-lazy
appear-vanish
arrival-departure
ascent-descent
asleep-awake
attack-defend
back-front
beautiful-ugly
before-after
begin-end
believe-doubt
beneficial-harmful
best-worst
bold-timid
bottom-top
bright-dull
busy-idle
calm-excited
cheerful-somber
clean-dirty
close-open
cold-hot
common-rare
complex-simple

comply-resist
crooked-straight
dark-light
day-night
decrease-increase
deep-shallow
defeat-victory
difficult-easy
down-up
dry-wet
early-late
easy-hard
empty-full
evil-good
exact-vague
exterior-interior
fancy-plain
far-near
fast-slow
first-last
flimsy-solid
foe-friend
foolish-wise
forget-remember
fragile-sturdy
fresh-stale
give-take
guilty-innocent
happy-sad
hard-soft
healthy-sick
heavy-light
high-low
include-omit

inferior-superior
join-separate
joy-grief
kind-cruel
large-small
leave-stay
long-short
loose-tight
lose-win
many-few
maximum-minimum
noisy-quiet
on-off
offense-defense
often-seldom
part-whole
permanent-temporary
plentiful-scarce
polite-rude
pull-push
regular-irregular
rich-poor
rough-smooth
save-spend
short-tall
shrink-swell
start-stop
strong-weak
tame-wild
thick-thin
true-false
usual-unusual
wide-narrow
zenith-nadir

Hundreds of Homonyms

acts, ax
ad, add
aerie, airy
aid, aide
ail, ale
air, err, heir
aisle, isle
all, awl
allowed, aloud
altar, alter
ant, aunt
arc, ark
ate, eight
auricle, oracle
aye, eye, I
bail, bale
bald, balled, bawled
band, banned
bare, bear
barren, baron
bass, base
be, bee
beach, beech
beat, beet
been, bin
bell, belle
berry, bury
berth, birth
better, bettor
billed, build
blew, blue
bloc, block
boar, bore
board, bored

bold, bowled
boll, bowl
bough, bow
bread, bred
bridal, bridle
buy, by
capital, capitol
carat (karat), carrot
cell, sell
cellar, seller
cent, scent, sent
cereal, serial
cheap, cheep
chews, choose
chili, chilly
chord, cord
chute, shoot
cite, sight, site
clause, claws
close, clothes
coarse, course
colonel, kernel
core, corps
counsel, council
creak, creek
currant, current
cymbal, symbol
dear, deer
descent, dissent
desert, dessert
dew, do, due
die, dye
doe, dough
dual, duel

ducked, duct
earn, urn
ewe, yew, you
eyelet, islet
faint, feint
fair, fare
faun, fawn
faze, phase
feat, feet
find, fined
fir, fur
flair, flare
flea, flee
flew, flu, flue
floe, flow
flour, flower
for, fore, four
foreword, forward
forth, fourth
foul, fowl
franc, frank
frays, phrase
friar, fryer
gait, gate
genes, jeans
gild, guild
gilt, guilt
gored, gourd
gorilla, guerrilla
grate, great
groan, grown
guessed, guest
guise, guys
hail, hale

Hundreds of Homonyms
(continued)

hair, hare
hall, haul
halve, have
hangar, hanger
hay, hey
heal, heel, he'll
hear, here
heard, herd
he'd, heed
hew, hue
hi, high
higher, hire
him, hymn
hoard, horde
hoarse, horse
hole, whole
hostel, hostile
hour, our
idle, idol
in, inn
jam, jamb
jinks, jinx
key, quay
knead, need
knew, new
knight, night
knot, not
know, no
lain, lane
laps, lapse
lead, led
leak, leek
lessen, lesson
lie, lye
links, lynx
load, lode
loan, lone
made, maid
mail, male
main, mane
maize, maze
mall, maul
manner, manor
marshal, martial
meat, meet, mete
medal, meddle, metal
might, mite
moan, mown
moose, mousse

muscle, mussel
naval, navel
nay, neigh
none, nun
oh, owe
one, won
or, ore
overdo, overdue
paced, paste
packed, pact
pail, pale
pain, pane
pair, pare, pear
palate, palette, pallet
pause, paws
peace, piece
peak, peek
peal, peel
pedal, peddle
peer, pier
pi, pie
plain, plane
plum, plumb
pole, poll
pore, pour
pray, prey
pride, pried
prince, prints
principal, principle
profit, prophet
quarts, quartz
rain, reign, rein
raise, rays
rap, wrap
read, red
read, reed
real, reel
right, write
ring, wring
road, rode
roe, row
root, route
rose, rows
rote, wrote
rough, ruff
rung, wrung

rye, wry
sac, sack
sail, sale
scene, seen
sea, see
seam, seem
serf, surf
sew, so, sow
shear, sheer
shone, shown
sighs, size
slay, sleigh
soar, sore
sole, soul
some, sum
son, sun
staid, stayed
stair, stare
stake, steak
stationary, stationery
steal, steel
step, steppe
straight, strait
suite, sweet
tail, tale
taper, tapir
taught, taut
tea, tee
team, teem
tear, tier
their, there, they're
threw, through
throne, thrown
thyme, time
to, too, two
toe, tow
vail, vale, veil
vain, vane, vein
wade, weighed
waist, waste
wait, weight
war, wore
ware, wear
we, wee
weak, week
who's, whose
wood, would
walk, wok
yoke, yolk

Parts of Speech

Part of Speech	Definition	Examples
noun	A noun is the name of a person, place, thing, or idea.	girl, man, Steve, cabin, pencil, happiness
verb	A verb expresses action or being.	sings, laughs, am, was, should
adjective	An adjective describes a noun or pronoun by telling how many, what kind, or which one.	five, few, beautiful, empty, that, those
adverb	An adverb describes a verb, adjective, or another adverb by telling how, when, or where.	slowly, carefully, soon, tomorrow, there
pronoun	A pronoun is used in place of a noun.	I, we, you, he, she, they, me, him, them, mine, someone
conjunction	A conjunction joins words, phrases, clauses, or sentences together.	and, but, also, however, therefore
preposition	A preposition shows the relationship between a noun or pronoun and another word.	about, around, before, behind, between, by, down, during, for, from, over, to
interjection	An interjection shows surprise or expresses strong feeling.	Ah! Help! Oh! Wow!

Rules of Punctuation

Use a *period*   ■

- after a sentence that is a statement or command.
- after an abbreviation.
- after an initial.

Use a *comma*   ,

- in a date to separate the day from the year and the year from the rest of the sentence.
- between words in a series.
- to set off *yes* and *no* at the beginning of a sentence.
- when giving a location or an address to separate the name of a city from the name of a state, the name of a state from the name of a country, and the name of a state or country from the rest of the sentence.
- before a conjunction when it joins two complete sentences.
- in direct address to separate the name of the person being spoken to from what is being said.
- to separate a quotation from the rest of the sentence unless a question mark or exclamation point is needed.
- after the greeting in a personal letter and after the closing in all letters.

Use a *question mark*   ?

- after a sentence that asks a question.
- after a question in a quotation.

Use an *exclamation point*   !

- after a sentence or a quotation that shows strong feeling.

Rules of Punctuation
(continued)

Use a *colon* :

- after the greeting in a business letter.

- at the beginning of a list of things in a sentence.

- to separate hours and minutes when writing times.

Use a *semicolon* ;

- in a compound sentence between principal clauses that are not joined by a conjunction.

Use an *apostrophe* '

- to show that one or more letters have been left out of a word.

- with *s* to form the possessive case of most singular nouns.

Use *quotation marks* " "

- before and after a quotation.

Use *parentheses* ( )

- to enclose parts of a sentence, such as explanations or comments, that could be omitted without making the sentence incomplete or changing its meaning.

Use a *hyphen* -

- at the end of a line in a word that is broken and continued on the following line.

- when dividing words into syllables for spelling or pronunciation purposes.

al-li-ga-tor

Rules for Forming Plurals

1. Most words are made plural by adding **s** to the singular form.

    cat   cats
    desk   desks

2. Words ending in **ch**, **s**, **sh**, **x**, and **z** are made plural by adding **es** to the singular form.

    box   boxes
    inch   inches

3. Most words ending in **y preceded by a vowel** are made plural by adding an **s**.

    monkey   monkeys
    tray   trays

4. Words ending in **y preceded by a consonant** are made plural by changing the **y** to **i** and adding **es**.

    penny   pennies
    bunny   bunnies

5. Words ending in **f** or **fe** are made plural by changing the **f** or **fe** to **v** and adding **es**.

    knife   knives
    thief   thieves

6. Some words ending in **f** are made plural by simply adding **s**.

    roof   roofs

7. Some words have **irregular plural forms**.

    deer   deer
    ox   oxen
    tooth   teeth

cat   cats

Great Ideas
For Using Hyphenated Words
and Compound Words on Pages 68-70

Hyphen Hunt

Have each student look through the dictionary and add as many hyphenated words as possible to the list on page 68. Then have students write stories incorporating as many of the words on their lists as they can.

Guess-a-Word

Have each student select ten hyphenated words from the list on page 68. For each word, have the student write a definition, omitting the hyphenated word. Tell students to exchange papers and fill in the omitted words.

Compound Capers

Have each student select ten compound words from the list on pages 69-70 to illustrate. Tell students to illustrate each word on a separate page of a booklet. Caution them not to write the word. Have students exchange finished booklets and guess the compound words.

Hyphenated Happenings

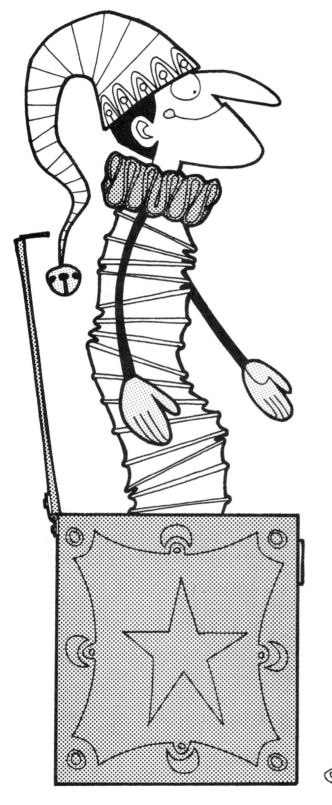

all-out
baby-sit
brand-new
brother-in-law
by-product
cold-blooded
cross-eyed
custom-built
deep-sea
double-cross
double-decker
drive-in
dry-clean
father-in-law
go-between
go-getter
grown-up
half-baked
half-mast
hide-and-seek
jack-in-the-box
jack-o'-lantern
life-size
light-footed
made-to-order
made-up
middle-aged
old-fashioned
one-half
one-sided
out-of-date
out-of-doors
pinch-hit
ping-pong
push-up
quick-tempered
right-handed
self-conscious
self-made
self-service
thin-skinned
third-rate
walkie-talkie
walk-up
would-be

Compound Capers

absentminded	bluegrass	eardrum
aftermath	breakfast	earmark
afternoon	bulldog	earthbound
airline	bullfight	earthquake
airmail	butterfly	eggnog
airplane	buttermilk	eggplant
airport	campfire	elsewhere
airstrip	candlestick	evergreen
airtight	cattleman	everyone
angelfish	chalkboard	everything
applesauce	chessboard	eyebrow
armband	classroom	eyelash
armchair	copyright	fairground
armhole	countdown	farmhand
backbone	courthouse	farmhouse
backfire	courtyard	farmland
background	crowbar	farmyard
backhand	cupcake	fingernail
bagpipe	daytime	fingerprint
bareback	deckhand	fireplace
barefoot	deerskin	fireworks
barnyard	dewdrop	foolproof
baseball	dodgeball	football
basketball	dogcart	footnote
battlefield	doorbell	forever
battleship	doormat	frostbite
birthday	doorway	fullback
birthmark	doubleheader	gaslight
birthplace	downpour	gatehouse
blackberry	downstream	gatekeeper
blackbird	downtown	glassware
blackboard	drainpipe	goldfish
blindfold	drawback	grapefruit
bluebird	drawbridge	grapevine
	drawstring	
	driftwood	
	drumstick	
	dugout	
	earache	

Compound Capers
(continued)

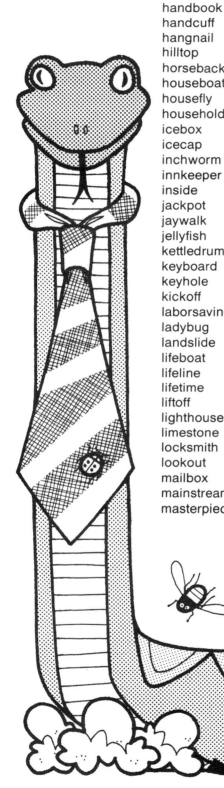

handbook	motorboat	rattlesnake
handcuff	motorcycle	roadside
hangnail	mouthpiece	roommate
hilltop	necktie	rosebud
horseback	nightfall	rowboat
houseboat	nightgown	runway
housefly	notebook	sandbox
household	offshore	scarecrow
icebox	outboard	scoutmaster
icecap	outguess	seafood
inchworm	outsmart	seashore
innkeeper	overcome	shipwreck
inside	overdue	shortstop
jackpot	overgrowth	starboard
jaywalk	overtime	steamboat
jellyfish	overweight	surfboard
kettledrum	paintbrush	tablespoon
keyboard	pancake	takeoff
keyhole	paperback	teaspoon
kickoff	paperweight	textbook
laborsaving	parkway	tightrope
ladybug	password	toothpick
landslide	peppercorn	trademark
lifeboat	pickpocket	tugboat
lifeline	pigtail	typewriter
lifetime	pillowcase	wallpaper
liftoff	pipeline	wastebasket
lighthouse	pitchfork	watermelon
limestone	popcorn	waterway
locksmith	postmark	wolfhound
lookout	quicksand	woodshed
mailbox	rainbow	woodwork
mainstream	raincoat	worldwide
masterpiece	raindrop	yardstick

Contraction Critter

Be

I'm	I am
you're	you are
he's	he is
she's	she is
it's	it is
we're	we are
they're	they are

Would

I'd	I would
you'd	you would
he'd	he would
she'd	she would
we'd	we would
they'd	they would

Will

I'll	I will
you'll	you will
he'll	he will
she'll	she will
it'll	it will
we'll	we will
they'll	they will
who'll	who will

Not

isn't	is not
aren't	are not
won't	will not
can't	cannot
wouldn't	would not
don't	do not
doesn't	does not
haven't	have not
hasn't	has not
hadn't	had not
shouldn't	should not
mightn't	might not
mustn't	must not
oughtn't	ought not
wasn't	was not
weren't	were not

Have

I've	I have
you've	you have
we've	we have
they've	they have

And more . . .

I'd	I had
he'd	he had
let's	let us
that's	that is
	that has
what's	what is
	what has
where's	where is
	where has
who's	who is
	who has

Word of the Week

adorn (ə - dôrń) *verb*—to add beauty to; decorate: *I will **adorn** my hat with ribbons.*

apathy (ap´- ə - thē) *noun*—lack of feeling or interest; indifference: *He was filled with **apathy** after losing his job.*

bawl (bôl) *verb*—to shout or cry loudly: *I heard her **bawl** when she cut her finger.*

bountiful (boun´- tə - fəl) *adj.*—more than enough; plentiful; abundant: *The farmer was proud of his **bountiful** crop.*

chasm (kaz´- əm) *noun*—deep opening or crack in the earth; gap; gorge: *We could not cross the wide **chasm**.*

condone (kən - dōń) *verb*—to forgive or overlook: *I cannot **condone** your bad manners.*

diligent (dil´- ə - jənt) *adj.*—steady and careful; hardworking and industrious: *She is a **diligent** student.*

dwindle (dwin´- dəl) *verb*—to become smaller or less; to shrink: *Lack of rain caused the water supply to **dwindle**.*

eccentric (ek - sen´- trik) *adj.*—different; odd; peculiar: *Everyone laughed at the **eccentric** woman who dyed her hair green.*

explicit (ek - splis´- ət) *adj.*—clearly expressed; distinctly stated; definite: *We found the house easily because of his **explicit** directions.*

flit (flit) *verb*—to move lightly and quickly from one place to another; dart: *We saw the hummingbird **flit** among the flowers.*

frivolous (friv´- ə - ləs) *adj.*—not serious; silly: ***Frivolous** behavior is out of place in a church or courtroom.*

Word of the Week
(continued)

girder (gur'- dər) *noun*—a large, horizontal beam of concrete, steel, or wood used as a main support: *The construction worker lowered the **girder** in place to support the floor.*

gnarled (närld) *adj.*—having a rough, twisted or knotted look: *There is a **gnarled** oak tree in the park. His leathery hands had been **gnarled** by time and hard work.*

heifer (hef'- ər) *noun*—a young cow that has not had a calf: *The **heifer** was grazing in the pasture.*

humiliate (hyo͞o - mil'- ē - āt) *verb*—make feel ashamed: *I will not **humiliate** you in front of your friends.*

impudent (im'- pyə - dənt) *adj.*—not well mannered; shamelessly bold; very rude: *The **impudent** student argued with the professor.*

isolate (ī'- sə - lāt) *verb*—separate from others; place or set apart: *It is wise to **isolate** patients with contagious diseases.*

jovial (jō'- vē - əl) *adj.*—full of fun; jolly: *The child was in a **jovial** mood on her birthday.*

jubilant (jo͞o'- bə - lənt) *adj.*—expressing or showing joy: *The team members were **jubilant**.*

katydid (kā'- tē - did) *noun*—a large, green grasshopper: *The **katydid** hopped on our grass.*

knoll (nōl) *noun*—a small, rounded hill; mound: *We had a picnic on the grassy **knoll**.*

loiter (loi'- tər) *verb*—stand around; linger idly: *Do not **loiter** in the halls.*

luminous (lo͞o'- mə - nəs) *adj.*—shining by its own light; full of light; bright: *The sun and stars are **luminous**.*

Word of the Week
(continued)

melancholy (mel′- ən - kol - ē) *adj.*—sad or gloomy; low in spirits: *She was in a **melancholy** mood.*

mumble (mum′ - bəl) *verb*—speak softly and unclearly: *If you **mumble**, I can't understand you.*

nimble (nim′- bəl) *adj.*—light and quick in movement; active and surefooted; agile: *The ballerina was graceful and **nimble**.*

noble (nō′- bəl) *adj.*—being of high birth, rank, or title; showing greatness of mind or character; possessing superior qualities, magnificent: *Although his beginning was humble his actions were **noble**.*

ominous (om′- ə - nəs) *adj.*—unfavorable; threatening; telling of bad luck or trouble to come: *The **ominous** clouds warned us that a storm was approaching.*

optional (op′- shə - nəl) *adj.*—not required; left to one's choice: *The chemistry class was **optional** for juniors.*

pulsate (pul′- sāt) *verb*—beat; throb; move rhythmically: *The frightened man's heart began to **pulsate** rapidly.*

punctual (pungk′ - chо͞о - əl) *adj.*—on time; prompt: *He makes a habit of being **punctual** no matter where he goes.*

quench (kwench) *verb*—put an end to by satisfying: *You can **quench** your thirst by drinking lemonade.*

querulous (kwer′- əl - əs) *adj.*—complaining; fretful: *The sick boy was very **querulous**.*

relic (rel′- ik) *noun*—a thing left from the past: *The vase was a **relic** from grandmother's day.*

rustic (rus′- tik) *adj.*—belonging to the country rather than the city; rural; simple, plain, unsophisticated: *They live in a **rustic** farmhouse.*

scant (skant) *adj.*—inadequate in size or amount; barely enough: *We had a **scant** supply of medicine.*

stifle (stī′- fəl) *verb*—to hold back; suppress; stop: *Vainly I tried to **stifle** my yawn.*

Word of the Week
(continued)

tapir (tā′ - pər) *noun*—a large piglike mammal with a long nose: *The **tapir** lives in tropical America and southern Asia.*

tedious (tē′ - dē - əs) *adj.*—long and tiring: *Her job on the assembly line was very **tedious**.*

uncanny (un - kan′ - ē) *adj.*—strange and mysterious: *He had an **uncanny** ability to predict the future.*

urban (ər′ - bən) *adj.*—having to do with cities or city life: *They missed their **urban** life-style when they moved to the farm.*

valiant (val′ - yənt) *adj.*—brave; courageous: *The fire fighter put up a **valiant** battle against the flames.*

verge (vərj) *noun*—the point at which something begins; brink; border: *She was on the **verge** of falling asleep when the phone rang.*

wilt (wilt) *verb*—droop or fade; become limp: *The delicate flower will **wilt** in this hot sun.*

witty (wit′ - ē) *adj.*—amusing in a clever way: *The comedian told a **witty** joke.*

xylem (zī′ - lem) *noun*—fleshy or woody part of plants: *The **xylem** carries water and minerals absorbed by the roots up to the plant.*

xylophone (zī′ - lə - fōn) *noun*—a musical instrument made of metal or wooden bars of varying lengths, which are sounded by striking: *She played the **xylophone** in the school band.*

yearn (yərn) *verb*—feel a deep desire or longing: *I **yearn** to go on a long vacation.*

yowl (youl) *noun*—long, loud wailing sound: *The **yowl** of the wolf could be heard through the forest.*

zeal (zēl) *noun*—eagerness; enthusiasm: *She worked with **zeal** on her science fair project.*

zephyr (zef′ - ər) *noun*—soft, gentle wind; mild breeze: *A **zephyr** blew across the plains.*

Great Ideas
For Using the Creative Writing Topics
Listed on Pages 77-81

Theme of the Week

Pick one of the topics, such as Animal Stories, as a theme for the week. Reproduce the list of suggested topics and post it at a creative writing center. Ask each student to choose a topic and to develop a short story based on that topic. Display completed stories on a bulletin board. Change the theme on a weekly or monthly basis.

Go Fish

Reproduce the list of suggested topics and cut the topics apart. Place them in a fish bowl, can, or box. Encourage students to "fish" for topics.

Howdy Partner

Have students work in pairs and collaborate on a story based on a selected topic.

Monthly Magazine

Start a monthly magazine featuring outstanding stories written from the suggested topics. Have students illustrate their stories. Share copies of the magazine in class and send them home for parents to enjoy.

Tape a Tale

Using a group of about six to eight students, select one topic. While you tape record, have one student begin a story based on the selected topic. When you give a signal, the next student continues the story, keeping the same main character and following the same story line until the signal is given again. Continue in this manner until each student has added to the story. Replay the tape for fun—and for other members of the class.

Spin a Story

Place one of the topic lists at a creative writing center. Make a wheel with a spinner as shown, numbering from one to twenty. Have students spin the spinner and write a story using the topic the arrow points to.

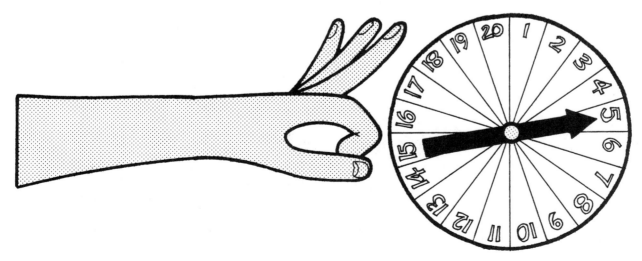

Creative Writing Topics
Sports

1. The Tryouts
2. My Turn at Bat
3. When the Crowds Went Wild
4. Scoring Secrets
5. Tops on the Team
6. How I Saved the Game
7. Slugger Strikes Out
8. The Day of the Championships
9. The Winning Goal
10. Super Stars
11. Bessie of Baseball Fame
12. Touchdown Troubles
13. On the Run
14. The Champ
15. The Soccer Star
16. The Stringers Meet the Wingers
17. The Play that Changed the Game
18. Race Against the Clock
19. How I Survived My Rookie Year
20. Newcomer to the Team

Creative Writing Topics
Mystery

1. The Fortune Cookie Caper

2. Super Spy for the FBI

3. Revenge of the Raven

4. A Scream in the Night

5. The Creature of Willow Creek

6. Up from the Deep

7. The Secret of Timber Tunnel

8. The Groaning Ghost

9. The Phone Booth Mystery

10. The Empty Room

11. Swamp Creature

12. The Monster That Took over the Earth

13. Happenings in the Haunted House

14. The Creepy Claw

15. The Nightmare

16. Not a Second Too Soon!

17. The Cave of the Dragon

18. The Case of the Stolen Key

19. Schoolroom Mystery

20. The Vanishing Footprints

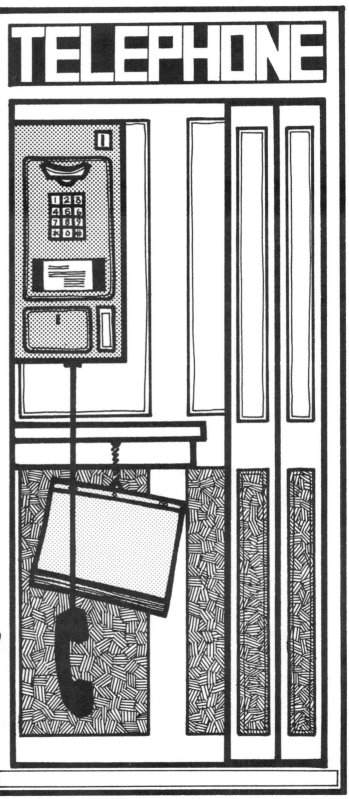

Creative Writing Topics
Animal Stories

1. Watson, the Worm
2. Horse Fever
3. The Blue Ribbon Pet
4. Puppy Power
5. A Turtle in Trouble
6. The Baboon That Loved Bubble Gum
7. The Empty Cage
8. Pet Problems
9. The Burglar and the Bear
10. The Pet Store Window
11. The Goofy Gopher
12. A Skunk in the Trunk
13. Rhino on the Run
14. A Visit to the Zoo
15. Pick of the Litter
16. The Laughing Lion
17. One Puppy Too Many
18. Horace, the Roller-Skating Hippo
19. Tale of the Giant Gorilla
20. Cat in the Candy Store

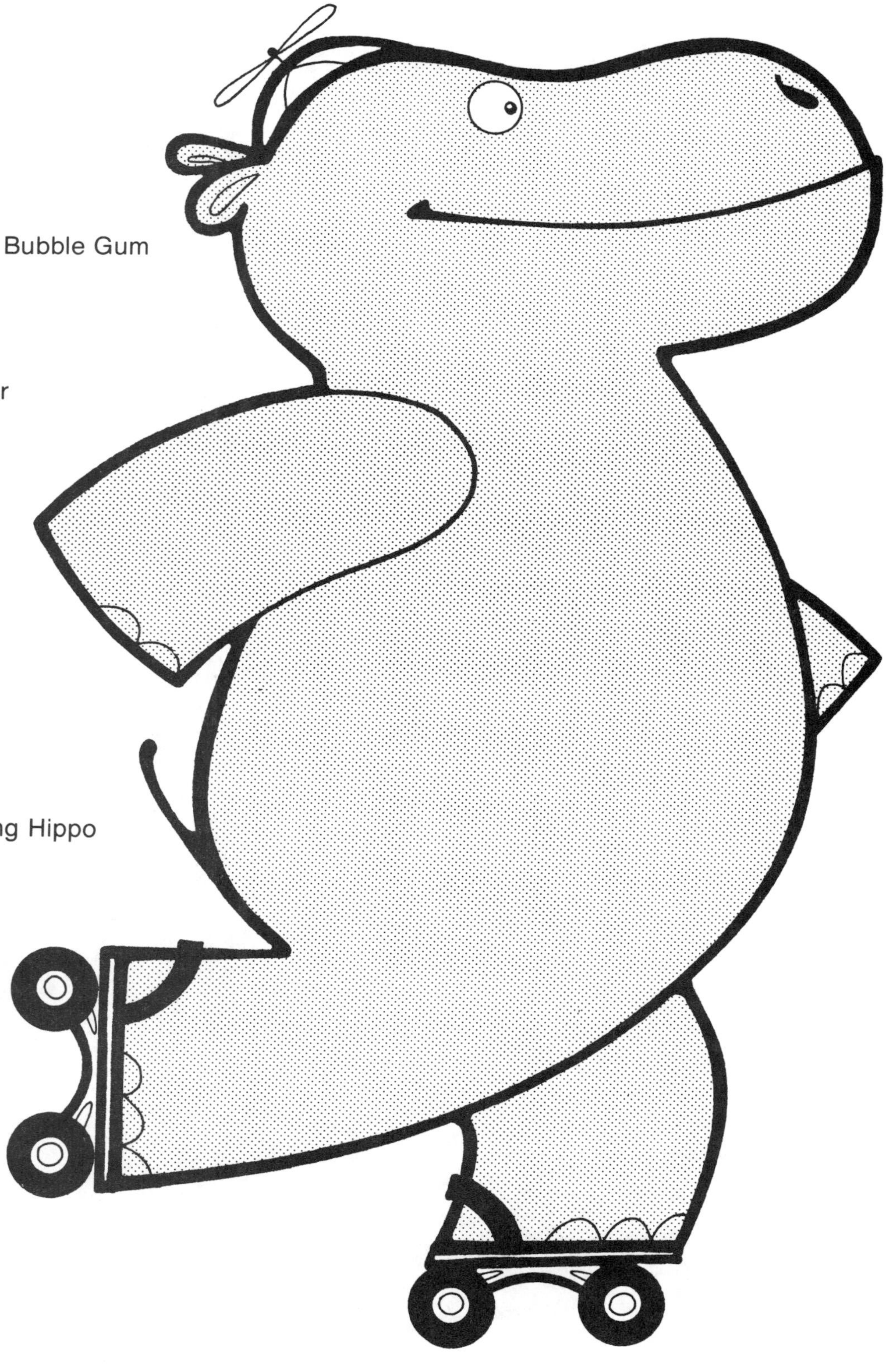

Creative Writing Topics
Just for Fun

1. Giggling Gus of Gatorville
2. The Magical Mirror
3. An Ingenious Invention
4. Mummy on the Loose
5. Wish Upon a Unicorn
6. The Whistling Wopperbopper
7. When Numbers Disappeared
8. A Glimpse of the Future
9. The Tri-Eyed Slitherwart
10. The Secret Formula of Dr. Ficklepickle
11. A Ride on the Rainbow
12. The Practical Joke
13. Backwards Day
14. The Blue Balloon Escape
15. The Purple House on Murple Street
16. Miss Mandy and the Candy Machine
17. A Cow on the Roof
18. The Surprise Package
19. The Chocolate Chip Gang
20. The Kid with the Green Face

Creative Writing Topics
General

1. Decisions, Decisions
2. Lost at Sea
3. A Special Secret
4. Conquer the Waves
5. To the Rescue
6. Wally, the Wizard
7. When the Sun Disappeared
8. A Kid in Trouble
9. The Spider That Grew and Grew
10. A Narrow Escape
11. Climb to the Peak
12. Without a Warning
13. On the Island of Goochie-Geechie
14. The Happiest Day
15. Trapped
16. The Hot-Air Balloon Ride
17. A Skunk in My Tub
18. Was I Ever Mad!
19. The Magical Ladder to Nowhere
20. Visitor from Another Planet

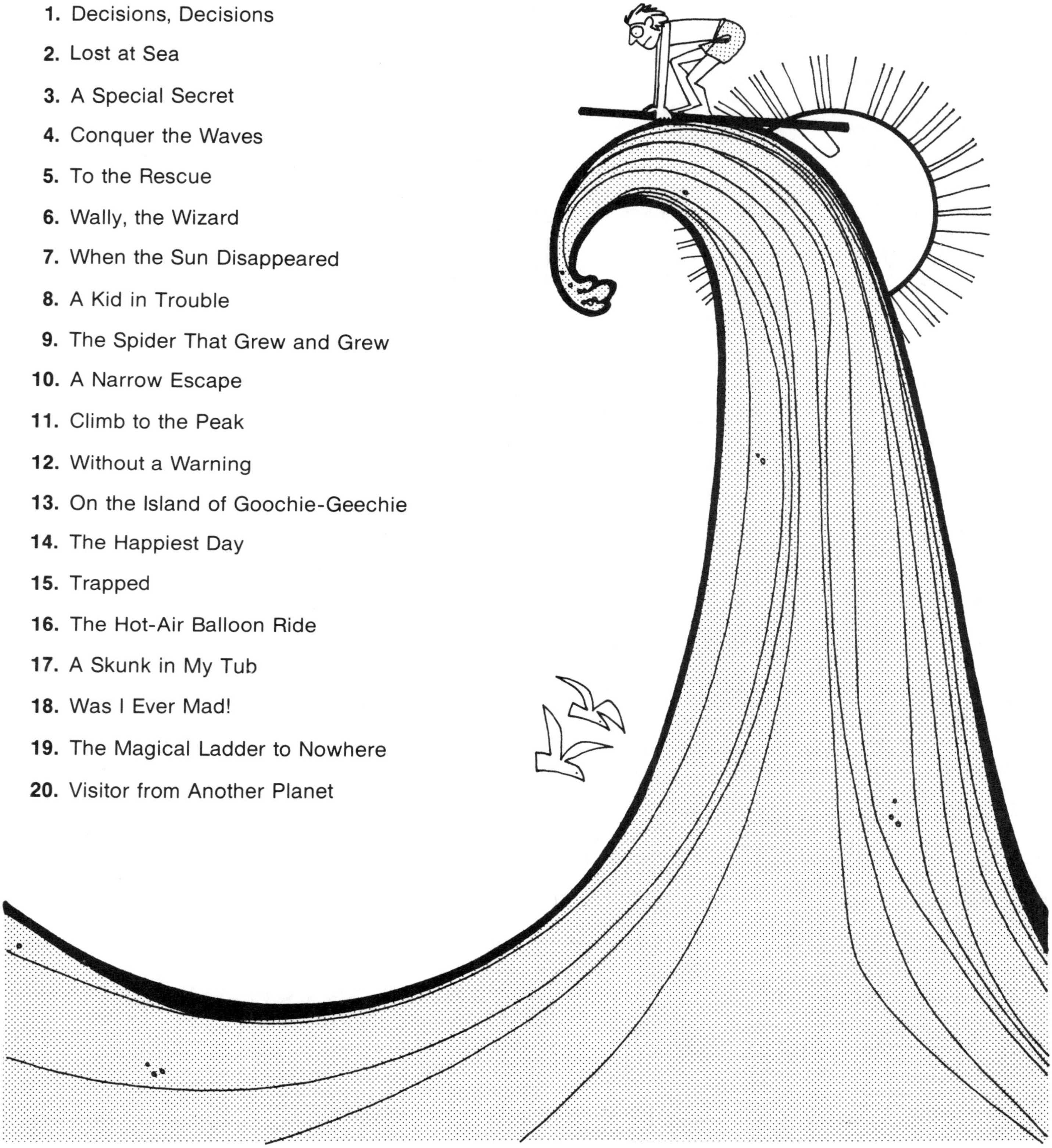

Book Report Brainstorms

Choose one of the following ways to share your book.

- Draw a cartoon strip of the most important events in the story.

- Make a soap, wood, or clay model to illustrate a character from the book.

- Write a different ending for the story.

- Make a list of questions you think everyone should be able to answer after reading the book.

- Make a diorama depicting the most exciting part of the book or the part you liked best.

- Compare a character in the story with a person you actually know. Write a paragraph or two in which you tell how they are alike and different.

- Make a word search puzzle using vocabulary words from the book.

- Make a time line of events in the story.

- Make a crossword puzzle using words from the book.

- Make a stitchery sampler to illustrate a scene from the book.

- Write a letter to a friend telling why you recommend the book.

- Pretend that you are the main character and write several diary pages describing an important event in the book.

- Make a shoe box filmstrip of an exciting event in the story.

- Use a wire coat hanger and string to make a mobile based on the book.

- Design a bookmark that tells something about the book.

- Make a poster to advertise the book.

- Write a one-act play based on the book.

- Make a puppet to represent a main character in the book.

- Tape record an interview in which you or a friend acts as the author of the book.

- Write a review of the book for a magazine or newspaper.

- Select and complete one of the forms on pages 83-85.

Name _____

Fiction Facts

Title _____

Author _____

Publisher _____

Type of Book _____ **Number of Pages** _____

Describe the main character.

_____

_____

_____

Describe a problem or difficulty the main character faces.

_____

_____

_____

Describe how the problem is solved.

_____

_____

_____

Give your opinion of the book.

_____

_____

_____

_____

_____

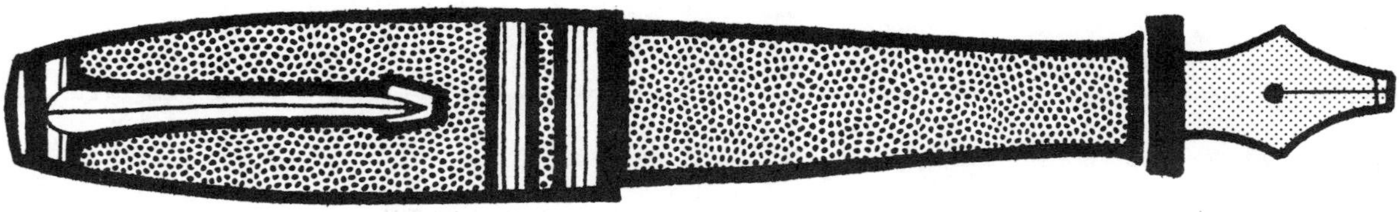

Read All About It Press

Vol. XXXIV, No. 4 _____, 19 ____ 35¢

Exciting New Book Announced

_____   _____
title   author

By _____
Staff Reporter

Focus on Main Characters

_____
_____
_____
_____
_____
_____

Exciting Plot Unfolds

_____
_____
_____
_____
_____
_____
_____

Portrait of Main Character

Here's What the Critics Say

_____
_____
_____
_____
_____
_____

Setting Is Super

_____
_____
_____
_____
_____
_____

This scene from the book shows _____

Name _____

Got the Plot?

Title _____

Author _____

Publisher _____

Type of Book _____ **Number of Pages** _____

1. **Introduction** (How does the book begin?)

_____

_____

_____

2. **Crisis** (What is the conflict or problem?)

_____

_____

3. **Rising Action** (How do the characters begin to solve the problem?)

_____

_____

4. **Climax** (What is the turning point of the story?)

_____

_____

_____

_____

5. **Falling Action** (How is the problem solved?)

_____

_____

6. **Resolution** (How does the story end?)

_____

_____

_____

The Dewey Decimal System
of
Classification

000-099   **General Works**
Bibliographies, General Encyclopedias, Reference Books

100-199   **Philosophy and Psychology**

200-299   **Religion**
Bible, Christian Religions, Other Religions, Greek and Roman Mythology

300-399   **Social Science**
Government, Community Life, Conservation, Transportation, Law, Holidays, Folk Tales, Fairy Tales and Legends, Costumes, Etiquette

400-499   **Language**
English Language, Study of Words, Alphabets, Dictionaries, Foreign Languages

500-599   **Science**
Mathematics, Astronomy, Physics, Chemistry, Geology, Prehistoric Life, Living Things

600-699   **Useful Arts, Technology, Applied Science**
The Body and Health, Safety, Machines and Inventions, Space and Aeronautics, Farming, Manufacturing, Building

700-799   **Fine Arts**
Architecture, Coins, Pottery, Drawing, Handicrafts, Painting, Photography, Music, Hobbies, Games, Sports, Magic

800-899   **Literature**
Poetry, Plays, Short Stories

900-999   **History**
History, Geography, Travel, Atlases, Biography

The Parts of a Book

Half-Title Page   The first printed page in a book and the page on which only the main part of the book title is listed. Both the subtitle and the author's name are omitted from this page.

Title Page   The second printed page in a book and the page on which the full title of the book, the name of the author, the name of the illustrator, and the name of the publisher are listed.

        author   the person who wrote the book
        illustrator the person who drew the pictures
        publisher the company that printed the book

Copyright Page   Usually the back of the title page, this page includes the copyright notice, the name of the person or publishing company holding the copyright, and the year in which the book was copyrighted.

Dedication Page   Page that carries a brief statement in which the author inscribes or addresses his book to someone as a way of recognizing or complimenting that person.

Table of Contents   A list of the significant parts of a book by title and page number in the order in which they appear. It is usually near the front of the book and includes the introduction, all chapter titles, the bibliography, and the index (if there is one).

Preface   A statement by the author telling how or why he or she wrote the book and acknowledging any help he or she had in doing so.

Introduction   An essay that sets the scene for the book, explains the subject or format of the book, or tells how to use the book.

Body or Text   The main part of the book.

Notes   Additional explanatory information about facts in the text or about the sources from which they have been gathered.

Glossary   An alphabetical listing of the difficult, special, or technical words used in a book with their definitions and, sometimes, their pronunciations.

Bibliography   A list of articles and other books referred to in the book or used by the author in writing it, or a list of writings relating to the same subject as the text. The works in a bibliography are usually arranged in alphabetical order based on the authors' last names.

Index   An alphabetical list of the names or topics covered in a book, together with the numbers of the pages on which they are defined, explained, or discussed. The index usually appears at the end of the book.

Name _____

My Vocabulary List

Here are some new words I have found while reading to add to my vocabulary.

Word	Part of Speech	Definition

waft ibis **yurt** **bask** jinx ekes
duct awry **ulna** ague **gawk**
bung **pyre** rote **zinc** **nary** hew
zeal veer flux
cowl

Bookmarks

Name _____

Pickled Plurals

Write the plural of each word. Use a dictionary if needed.

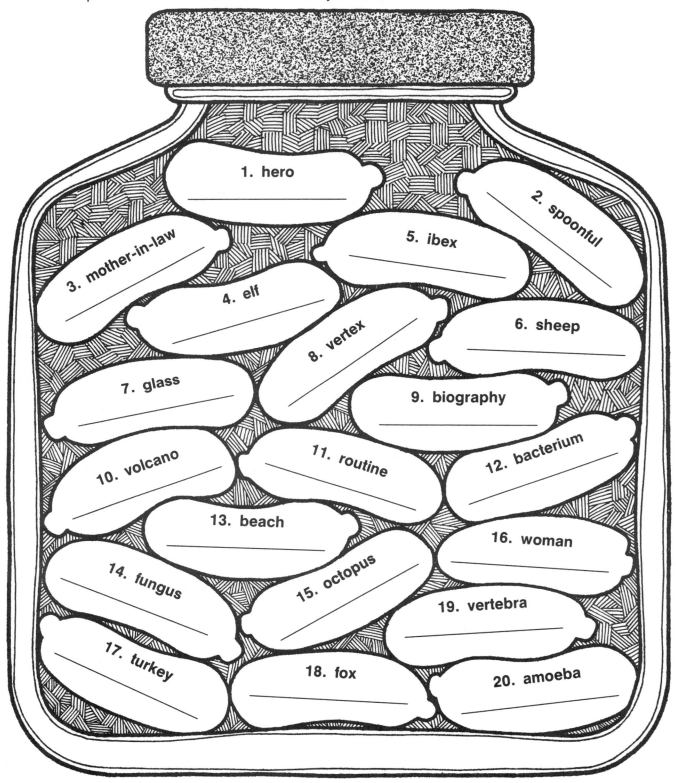

1. hero

2. spoonful

3. mother-in-law

4. elf

5. ibex

6. sheep

7. glass

8. vertex

9. biography

10. volcano

11. routine

12. bacterium

13. beach

14. fungus

15. octopus

16. woman

17. turkey

18. fox

19. vertebra

20. amoeba

Name _____

Create a Word

1. Make up a new word. (Check in the dictionary to be sure that your word is *not* listed.)

2. Write your word in large letters across the top of a piece of white art paper.

3. Divide your word into syllables, mark the long vowels, and show where the accent mark belongs so that others will know how to pronounce your word.

4. Write the correct part of speech (noun, verb, adjective, or adverb) for your word.

5. Draw a picture of your word.

6. Write a definition or tell what your word means in one or two sentences.

7. Use your word in a sentence and underline your new word.

messikinder
(mes' - si - kin - dər) *noun*

a messy child
The <u>messikinder</u> has a great time playing in the mud.

Name _____

Spelling Riddle

Find the letter in front of the correct spelling of each word, and write it on the line at the bottom of the page to solve the riddle: **Where does a lamb go when it needs a haircut?** The first one has been done for you.

1.	**s** gramar	**b** grammer	**t** grammar
2.	**o** separate	**a** seperate	**e** sepurate
3.	**r** accomodate	**t** accommodate	**e** acommodate
4.	**h** business	**n** bisiness	**o** busines
5.	**b** embarras	**o** embarass	**e** embarrass
6.	**s** miscellanious	**r** missellaneous	**b** miscellaneous
7.	**a** familiar	**s** familar	**g** famillure
8.	**a** experience	**r** expereince	**j** expireance
9.	**n** judggment	**l** judgemint	**b** judgment
10.	**k** surprize	**a** surprise	**j** sirprise
11.	**b** occured	**y** ocurred	**a** occurred
12.	**s** necessary	**t** necesery	**i** neccessery
13.	**h** leisure	**e** leezure	**y** liesure
14.	**c** lisence	**d** licenze	**o** license
15.	**p** excellent	**e** exsellent	**a** excellant

t _ _ _ _ _   _ _ _   _ _ _ _

Name _____

What Would You Do With . . . ?

Use a dictionary to find the meanings of these words. Write each word under the proper heading.

What would you do with a/an

- ambrosia
- aspic
- beret
- calliope
- celesta
- escargot
- fife
- jicama
- monocle
- ocarina
- papaya
- peplum

- pumpernickel
- snood
- spinet
- tiara
- timbrel
- tippet
- tofu
- toga
- tutu
- tympani
- vichyssoise
- zither

Eat It	Wear It	Play It

Hat Happenings

1. Choose one hat below and decide who wears it.

2. Write a short story about an adventure the hat wearer has.

3. Draw a large picture of the hat you chose.

4. Mount your completed story on the hat.

5. Add your hat to our Hat Happenings bulletin board.

Name _____

Cross Country Cryptogram

In this puzzle you have a riddle question and its answer, but they are in code. The letters in the question and those in the answer stand for other letters. Can you figure out what letters the code letters stand for?

The name of a city, SAN FRANCISCO, has been filled in. Look at the S in SAN. It is under the W. That means that in this code, W stands for S. At the bottom of the page, write S under the letter W. Then look for other W's in the question and the answer. Write S under any W that you find.

Follow these steps for every letter in SAN FRANCISCO. Then start guessing some of the other missing letters in the cryptogram.

Question: Y B N E   Q U P W   N C C

___ ___ ___ ___   ___ ___ ___ ___   ___ ___ ___

E B P   Y N Z   H K U T

___ ___ ___   ___ ___ ___   ___ ___ ___ ___

J P Y   Z U K S   E U

___ ___ ___   ___ ___ ___ ___   ___ ___

W N J   H K N J O R W O U
<u>S</u> <u>A</u> <u>N</u>   <u>F</u> <u>R</u> <u>A</u> <u>N</u> <u>C</u> <u>I</u> <u>S</u> <u>C</u> <u>O</u>

Y R E B U X E   T U L R J Q ?

___ ___ ___ ___ ___ ___ ___   ___ ___ ___ ___ ___ ___ ?

Answer: K N R C K U N A   E K N O S W

___ ___ ___ ___ ___ ___ ___ ___   ___ ___ ___ ___ ___ ___

**Coded
Letters:** A B C D E F G H I J K L M

___ ___ ___ ___ ___ ___ ___ ___ ___ ___ ___ ___ ___

N O P Q R S T U V W X Y Z

___ ___ ___ ___ ___ ___ ___ ___ ___ ___ ___ ___ ___

Name _____

The Case of the Missing Masterpiece

A valuable oil painting was discovered missing from the Museum of Modern Art shortly after a tour group left. Although each person in the group vehemently denied taking the painting, the police reasoned that the last person to leave the museum was the culprit. Solve the mystery by using the clues given below to discover who was the last person to leave. Beside each name write the actual time that person left the museum.

_____ **Susie Shultz** left twenty minutes before Sylvia Spencer.

_____ **Sammy Slade** left fifteen minutes after Stanley Slater.

_____ **Sally Shepard** left fifty minutes before Susie Shultz.

_____ **Sylvia Spencer** left thirty-five minutes after Sammy Slade.

_____ **Sid Sharp** left fifteen minutes before five o'clock.

_____ **Samantha Strand** left twenty-five minutes after Susie Shultz.

_____ **Stanley Slater** left twenty minutes before Sid Sharp.

_____ **Sylvester Scruggs** left forty-five minutes before Sammy Slade.

_____ **Simon Sweeney** left ten minutes before Samantha Strand.

The thief was _____ .

Samantha Strand   Simon Sweeney   Sally Shepard   Sammy Slade

Sid Sharp   Susie Shultz   Stanley Slater   Sylvia Spencer   Sylvester Scruggs

Math

Addition Table

+	0	1	2	3	4	5	6	7	8	9	10	11	12
0	0	1	2	3	4	5	6	7	8	9	10	11	12
1	1	2	3	4	5	6	7	8	9	10	11	12	13
2	2	3	4	5	6	7	8	9	10	11	12	13	14
3	3	4	5	6	7	8	9	10	11	12	13	14	15
4	4	5	6	7	8	9	10	11	12	13	14	15	16
5	5	6	7	8	9	10	11	12	13	14	15	16	17
6	6	7	8	9	10	11	12	13	14	15	16	17	18
7	7	8	9	10	11	12	13	14	15	16	17	18	19
8	8	9	10	11	12	13	14	15	16	17	18	19	20
9	9	10	11	12	13	14	15	16	17	18	19	20	21
10	10	11	12	13	14	15	16	17	18	19	20	21	22
11	11	12	13	14	15	16	17	18	19	20	21	22	23
12	12	13	14	15	16	17	18	19	20	21	22	23	24

Blank Addition Table

+	0	1	2	3	4	5	6	7	8	9	10	11	12
0													
1													
2													
3													
4													
5													
6													
7													
8													
9													
10													
11													
12													

Multiplication Table

×	0	1	2	3	4	5	6	7	8	9	10	11	12
0	0	0	0	0	0	0	0	0	0	0	0	0	0
1	0	1	2	3	4	5	6	7	8	9	10	11	12
2	0	2	4	6	8	10	12	14	16	18	20	22	24
3	0	3	6	9	12	15	18	21	24	27	30	33	36
4	0	4	8	12	16	20	24	28	32	36	40	44	48
5	0	5	10	15	20	25	30	35	40	45	50	55	60
6	0	6	12	18	24	30	36	42	48	54	60	66	72
7	0	7	14	21	28	35	42	49	56	63	70	77	84
8	0	8	16	24	32	40	48	56	64	72	80	88	96
9	0	9	18	27	36	45	54	63	72	81	90	99	108
10	0	10	20	30	40	50	60	70	80	90	100	110	120
11	0	11	22	33	44	55	66	77	88	99	110	121	132
12	0	12	24	36	48	60	72	84	96	108	120	132	144

Name _____

Blank Multiplication Table

×	0	1	2	3	4	5	6	7	8	9	10	11	12
0													
1													
2													
3													
4													
5													
6													
7													
8													
9													
10													
11													
12													

Name _____

The Sum's the Same

In these squares, the sum's the same whether you add the numbers across a row, down a column, or along a diagonal. Fill in the missing numbers in square 1.

1.

	16	
14		10

1. The sum is 24.

In squares 2 and 3, fill in the missing numbers and identify the sums.

2.

9		
	11	15
17		

2. The sum is _____ .

3.

10	20	
	12	
		14

3. The sum is _____ .

In square 4, the numbers are 1, 3, 5, 7, 9, 11, 13, 15, and 17. Can you arrange them in the boxes so that they sum to 27 across each row, down each column, and along each diagonal?

4.

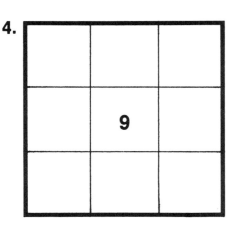

Name _____

How Strong Is Your Addition?

Find the sums.

	a	b	c	d	e
1	2 4 + 5	3 6 + 8	9 7 + 4	8 5 + 6	7 2 + 3
2	14 + 23	25 + 36	55 + 89	72 + 47	63 + 79
3	506 + 36	352 + 95	819 + 85	247 + 76	708 + 55
4	83 36 + 45	72 51 + 99	35 67 + 48	87 92 + 73	96 34 + 21
5	287 + 690	731 + 564	800 + 787	909 + 472	553 + 685

25 correct

20-24 correct

15-19 correct

10-14 correct

5-9 correct

0-4 correct

Count your correct answers, and mark your score.

Name _____

Find Five Subtraction Quiz

Find and circle the five incorrect answers below.

	a	b	c	d	e
1	26 - 8 18	17 - 9 8	31 - 4 27	54 - 7 46	21 - 9 12
2	32 - 18 14	45 - 27 18	22 - 14 7	53 - 24 29	68 - 48 20
3	102 - 36 66	271 - 84 187	318 - 49 269	205 - 55 150	522 - 37 483
4	428 - 163 265	519 - 236 283	857 - 189 668	706 - 358 348	625 - 471 134
5	5001 - 3112 1889	6315 - 1828 4487	3068 - 1219 1849	7000 - 3423 3377	9012 - 3687 5325

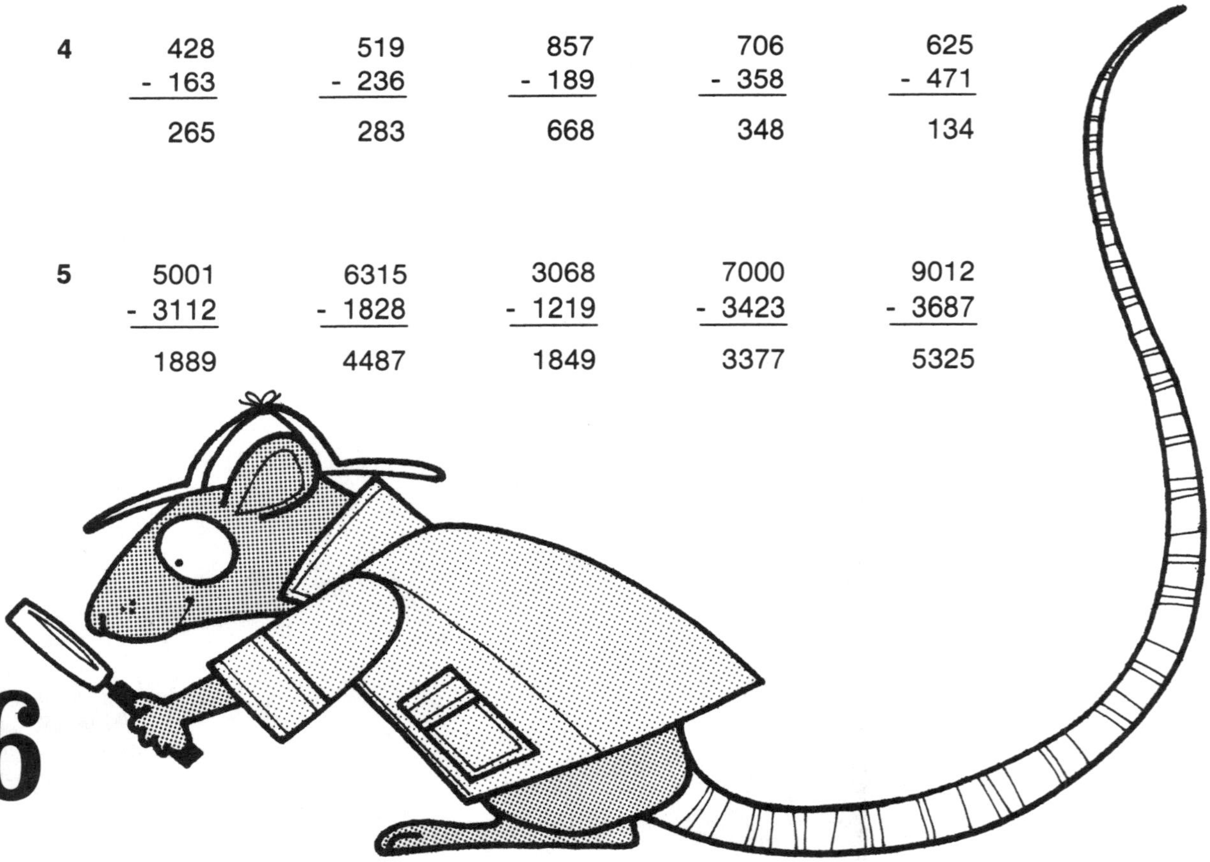

66

Name _____

Multiplication Quiz

Find the products.

	a	b	c	d	e
1	6 × 7	8 × 8	9 × 7	5 × 6	7 × 8
2	13 × 4	26 × 8	34 × 9	58 × 9	63 × 7
3	27 × 18	55 × 32	40 × 26	73 × 45	81 × 57
4	106 × 28	300 × 52	411 × 87	639 × 76	885 × 62
5	226 × 118	602 × 778	558 × 691	723 × 364	982 × 352

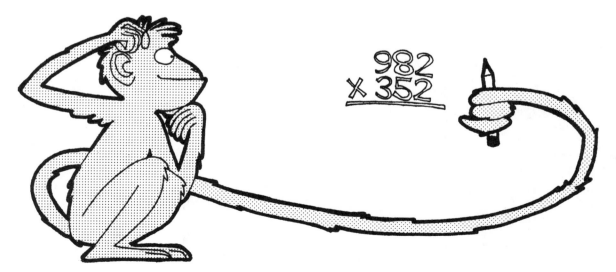

Name _____

Doughnuts Division

Find the quotients.

	a	b	c	d	e
1	4)52	8)208	9)306	9)522	7)441
2	18)486	32)1,760	26)1,040	73)3,285	57)4,617
3	35)672	63)154	27)389	95)585	76)461
4	105)2,968	301)1,560	312)3,575	639)4,856	832)5,487

Listen carefully as your teacher reads the answers. Put a check mark beside each one that is wrong. Count the number of problems you did right. Give yourself five points for each correct answer. Figure your score on the lines below.

Number right _____ x 5 = _____

Then use the doughnut menu to see how your division rates.

Doughnut Menu

100	*the works*
80 through 99	*jelly-filled*
60 through 79	*chocolate-covered*
40 through 59	*glazed*
20 through 39	*plain*
below 20	*only a hole*

Graphs Galore

A **graph** is a line or diagram that shows how one quantity depends on or changes with another. A graph shows a comparison or system of relationships in a way that is easy to understand. Among the various kinds of graphs are **bar graphs**, **picture graphs**, **line graphs**, and **circle graphs**.

Bar Graph

FAVORITE PETS OF THE STUDENTS IN ROOM 6	0	5	10	15
Dogs				
Cats				
Hamsters				
Parakeets				
Rabbits				
Guinea Pigs				
Chickens				
Hermit Crabs				
Snakes				
Fish				
Horses				

Picture Graph

MAJOR SHEEP-RAISING COUNTRIES OF THE WORLD

Each 🐑 stands for one million sheep.

Australia
New Zealand
South Africa
Peru
Iraq
Uruguay
Mongolia
Yemen

Line Graph

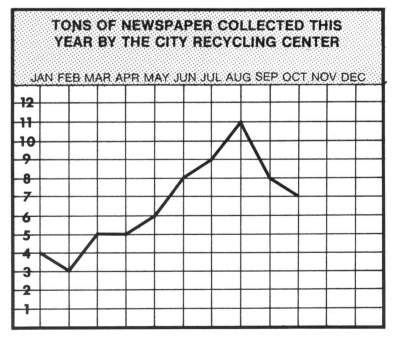

TONS OF NEWSPAPER COLLECTED THIS YEAR BY THE CITY RECYCLING CENTER

JAN FEB MAR APR MAY JUN JUL AUG SEP OCT NOV DEC

Circle Graph

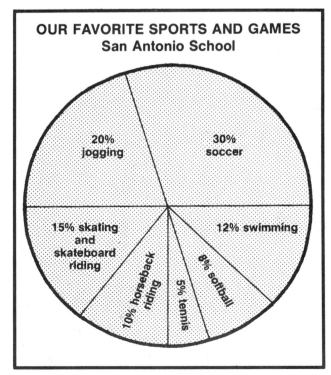

OUR FAVORITE SPORTS AND GAMES
San Antonio School

20% jogging
30% soccer
15% skating and skateboard riding
12% swimming
10% horseback riding
5% tennis
8% softball

Name _____

More Graphs Galore

Using the graphs on page 107, answer these questions.

Bar Graph

1. Which is the most popular pet in room 6? _____

2. Which is the least popular pet on the graph? _____

3. Do more students like hamsters or chickens? _____

4. How many students like parakeets? _____

Picture Graph

1. How many sheep can be found in South Africa? _____

2. Which country raises the most sheep? _____

3. Which three countries raise the same amount of sheep? _____

4. How many more sheep are raised in New Zealand than in South Africa? _____

Line Graph

1. In which month was the most newspaper collected? _____

2. In which month was the least amount collected? _____

3. How many tons of newspaper were collected in July? _____

4. Was more newspaper collected in October or May? _____

Circle Graph

1. What is the most popular sport at San Antonio School? _____

2. According to the graph, which is the least popular sport? _____

3. Which sport is more popular, swimming or jogging? _____

4. Which two sports make up half of the favorites at San Antonio School? _____

Social Studies

Ideas for Social Studies Projects

Diorama

Have students pick topics from the list on page 111 and do research on these topics. Then tell them to make shoe box dioramas depicting their topics and to write one-page summaries of their most important findings.

Roll a Scroll

Have students pick topics from the list on page 111 and do research on their topics. Then have them make pictorial scrolls with a brief caption or description for each picture. Cut a screen-sized opening in one side of a cardboard box. Mount each scroll on dowels so that it can be rolled past this opening. Have students explain frames as they are displayed.

Fact Cubes

Tell students to pick topics from the list on page 111 and research them thoroughly. Then have students cover grocery boxes with colored paper (butcher, construction, shelf, or wrapping paper) and fill all six sides with interesting information and pictures about their topics. If appropriate, suggest that students devote one side to each of six aspects of their topics. Display cubes in the classroom for other students to read and enjoy.

Make a Model

Have students pick topics from the list on page 111 and research them thoroughly. Then suggest that students use cardboard, clay, papier mâché, popsicle sticks, soap, sugar cubes, or other appropriate media to construct models related to the topics they have studied. Where possible, models should be ones that work or ones that can be used to demonstrate something students have learned.

Perfect Pantomime

Divide the class into groups of two to four. Assign or allow each group to select a topic from the list on page 111. Tell group members that they are to do research on their chosen topics. Have them decide on a series of actions to use in portraying some important facts they have learned and write a narration explaining these actions. When the productions are presented to the class, one group member should narrate while the others pantomime.

Skinny Skit

Divide the class into groups of two to four. Assign or allow each group to select a topic from the list on page 111. Tell group members that they are to do research on their chosen topics and then are to present a short, or "skinny," skit in which they share some facts they have learned with other members of the class. Encourage them to be creative in their use of hats, props, and simple costumes.

Meeting of the Minds

Divide the class into groups of three or four. Assign or allow each group to select a topic from the list on page 111. Tell the members of these groups that they are to do research on their chosen topics and then are to present a television game or interview show complete with host and guests. Guests should wear costumes, carry props, and come prepared to play the parts of people related to the group's topic.

Fifty Nifty Topics
for
Social Studies Research

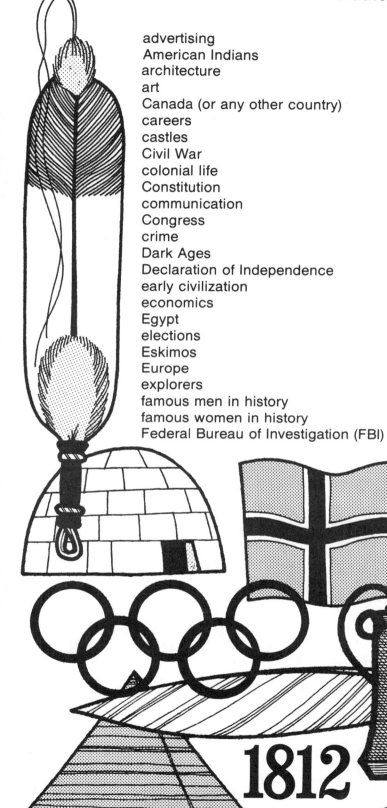

advertising
American Indians
architecture
art
Canada (or any other country)
careers
castles
Civil War
colonial life
Constitution
communication
Congress
crime
Dark Ages
Declaration of Independence
early civilization
economics
Egypt
elections
Eskimos
Europe
explorers
famous men in history
famous women in history
Federal Bureau of Investigation (FBI)

Florida (or any other state)
French Revolution
geography
Hellenic Age
maps
Middle East
national parks
Olympics
pioneers
pony express
presidents
Renaissance
Revolutionary War
stock market
Stone Age
Supreme Court
transportation
underground railroad
United Nations
voyages and discoveries
War of 1812
westward movement
White House
world neighbors
world of the future

Map of the United States

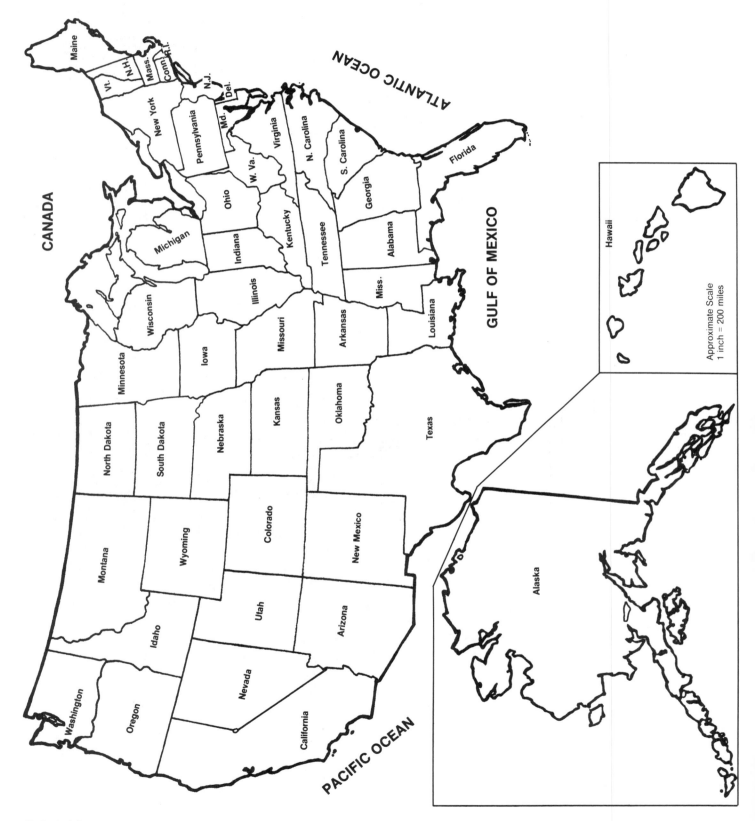

Map Quiz

Using the map of the United States on page 112, answer these questions.

1. Which is the smallest state? _____

2. Name the three largest states in order of their size.

   1st _____ **2nd** _____ **3rd** _____

3. What state is bordered on the north by Nebraska, on the east by Missouri, on the south by

   Oklahoma, and on the west by Colorado? _____

4. Which state is farther west, Montana or Wyoming? _____

5. Which states border California? _____

6. What state lies directly north of Illinois? _____

7. In the continental United States, what state has the least number of states on its borders?

   _____

8. In the continental United States, what state has the longest north-south boundary?

   _____

9. What six states border Idaho? _____

   _____

10. Which state is farther south, Louisiana or Texas? _____

11. Which is the only state completely surrounded by water? _____

12. Which state is bounded on the north by Illinois, Indiana, and Ohio? _____

    _____

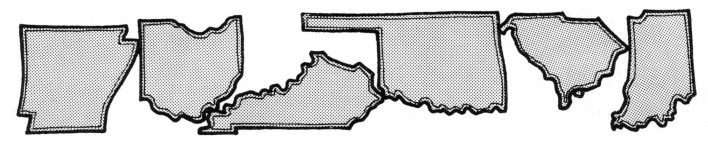

Abbreviations for State Names

State Name	Standard Abbreviation	Two-Letter Abbreviation*
Alabama	Ala.	AL
Alaska	Alaska	AK
Arizona	Ariz.	AZ
Arkansas	Ark.	AR
California	Calif.	CA
Colorado	Colo.	CO
Connecticut	Conn.	CT
Delaware	Del.	DE
Florida	Fla.	FL
Georgia	Ga.	GA
Hawaii	Hawaii	HI
Idaho	Idaho	ID
Illinois	Ill.	IL
Indiana	Ind.	IN
Iowa	Iowa	IA
Kansas	Kans.	KS
Kentucky	Ky.	KY
Louisiana	La.	LA
Maine	Maine	ME
Maryland	Md.	MD
Massachusetts	Mass.	MA
Michigan	Mich.	MI
Minnesota	Minn.	MN
Mississippi	Miss.	MS
Missouri	Mo.	MO
Montana	Mont.	MT
Nebraska	Nebr.	NE
Nevada	Nev.	NV
New Hampshire	N.H.	NH
New Jersey	N.J.	NJ
New Mexico	N.Mex.	NM
New York	N.Y.	NY
North Carolina	N.C.	NC
North Dakota	N.Dak.	ND
Ohio	Ohio	OH
Oklahoma	Okla.	OK
Oregon	Oreg.	OR
Pennsylvania	Pa.	PA
Rhode Island	R.I.	RI
South Carolina	S.C.	SC
South Dakota	S.Dak.	SD
Tennessee	Tenn.	TN
Texas	Tex.	TX
Utah	Utah	UT
Vermont	Vt.	VT
Virginia	Va.	VA
Washington	Wash.	WA
West Virginia	W.Va.	WV
Wisconsin	Wis.	WI
Wyoming	Wyo.	WY

* Specified by the United States government for use with zip codes.

Map of Canada

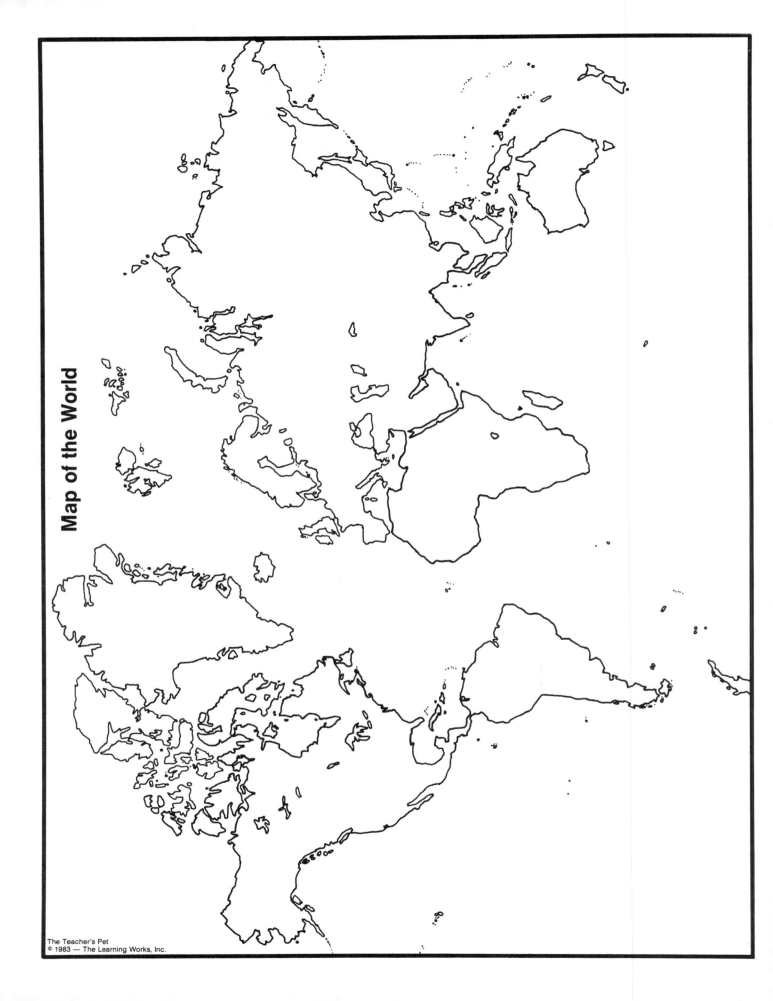

Map of the World

Social Studies

Name _____

Where in the World Are You From?

Talk with your mom and dad to find out where your parents, grandparents, great-grandparents, and great-great-grandparents came from. Use this information to fill in the worksheet below. Make a key in which you use a different color for each relative. Then color the map on page 116 to show where your ancestors came from.

	Dad's Family	**Mom's Family**
My grandmother came from	_____	_____
My grandfather came from	_____	_____
My grandmother's mother came from	_____	_____
My grandmother's father came from	_____	_____
My grandfather's mother came from	_____	_____
My grandfather's father came from	_____	_____
My grandmother's mother's mother came from	_____	_____
My grandmother's mother's father came from	_____	_____
My grandmother's father's mother came from	_____	_____
My grandmother's father's father came from	_____	_____
My grandfather's mother's mother came from	_____	_____
My grandfather's mother's father came from	_____	_____
My grandfather's father's mother came from	_____	_____
My grandfather's father's father came from	_____	_____

Name _____

My Family Tree

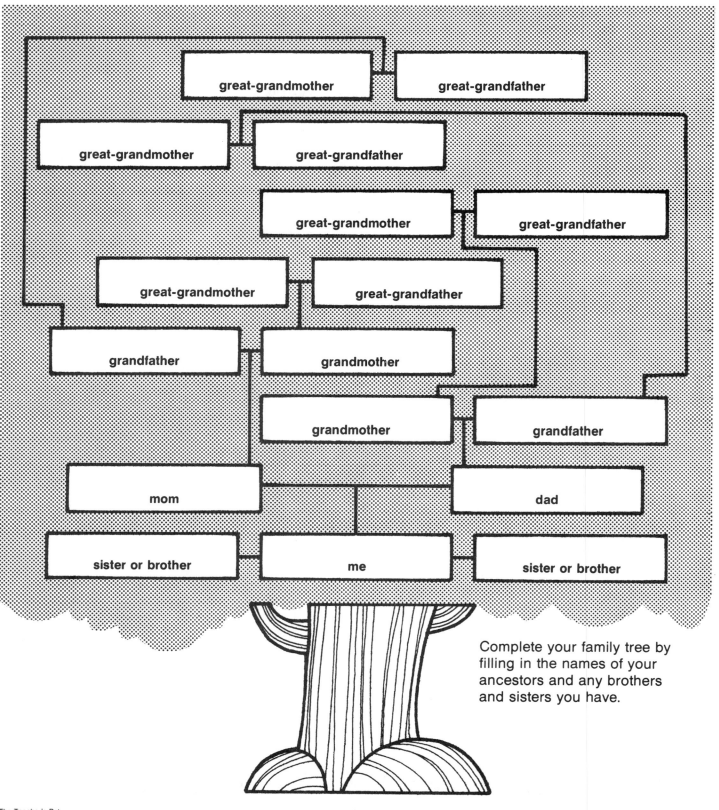

great-grandmother

great-grandfather

great-grandmother

great-grandfather

great-grandmother

great-grandfather

great-grandmother

great-grandfather

grandfather

grandmother

grandmother

grandfather

mom

dad

sister or brother

me

sister or brother

Complete your family tree by filling in the names of your ancestors and any brothers and sisters you have.

Name _____

People Posters

1. Think about famous people in such fields as politics, science, sports, entertainment, and the arts. Select one woman or man whom you would like to learn more about. Here are some suggestions:

Jane Addams	Margot Fonteyn	Rudolph Nureyev
Louisa May Alcott	Stephen Foster	Louis Pasteur
Hans Christian Andersen	Benjamin Franklin	Luciano Pavarotti
Tracy Austin	Mohandas Karamchand Gandhi	Anna Pavlova
Ludwig van Beethoven	Steve Garvey	Pablo Picasso
Irving Berlin	George Gershwin	Cole Porter
E. Power Biggs	Dorothy Hamill	Jackie Robinson
Ralph Bunche	Helen Keller	Will Rogers
Marie Curie	John F. Kennedy	Artur Rubinstein
Charles Dickens	Martin Luther King, Jr.	Albert Schweitzer
Thomas Alva Edison	Margaret Mead	Beverly Sills
Albert Einstein	Ralph Nader	Harriet Tubman

2. Read about the person you have selected and take notes on important facts.

3. Use these facts to write a report two or three pages long. Write it as if *you* were the person you selected.

4. Draw and color a picture of the person you chose or an important event in that person's life.

5. Write the person's name in large letters across the top of a 12-inch-by-18-inch piece of colored construction paper.

6. Paste the picture on one side of the construction paper and staple the report next to it.

7. Display your People Poster for other class members to enjoy.

Variation: Bind all of the People Posters together to make a class album.

Name _____

Research a Country

1. Pick the stamp of a country from page 121 or 122. This is your country to investigate.

2. Using encyclopedias, magazines, and other reference materials, find the answers to the following questions:

   a. What are the names and locations of three important cities in this country?

   b. What are some favorite foods of this country? Describe them.

   c. What is the weather like in this country?

   d. What type of government does this country have? How does it differ from the government of the country you live in?

   e. Describe the means of transportation used in this country.

   f. Name and describe three types of sports or recreation enjoyed by the people of this country.

   g. How is education in this country different from or similar to that in the country you live in?

   h. How do people dress in this country? Draw an illustration.

   i. List and describe three places of interest a tourist should visit in this country.

   j. What does this country look like? Draw a map and include cities, mountains, lakes, rivers, deserts, and other important geographical features.

   k. How do the houses and buildings in this country differ from those you are familiar with?

   l. What is the name of an important leader of this country today?

   m. What are the primary resources of this country?

   n. What products does this country export?

3. When all of your facts have been gathered, organize them and bind them in a notebook.

4. Decorate the notebook cover using an enlarged picture of your stamp, or design something entirely different.

5. Add illustrations, pictures, charts, and newspaper articles about this country today.

Stamps for Research a Country

Stamps for Research a Country
(continued)

Latitude and Longitude

We often need a way to describe where places are on the earth. To help us, mapmakers have created a system of lines. Some of these lines run east and west. Others of these lines run north and south.

The lines that run east and west are called **parallels**, or lines of **latitude**. Parallels never meet. They are used to measure the distance north or south of the **equator**.

The lines that run north and south are called **meridians**, or lines of **longitude**. Meridians meet at the North Pole and at the South Pole. They are used to measure the distance east or west of a reference line called the **prime meridian**.

Mapmakers have given these lines number names. The equator is 0° (we say *zero degrees*) latitude. The other parallels are numbered to show how far north or south they are. The prime meridian is 0° longitude. The other meridians are numbered to show how far east or west they are.

Using the map above, locate the cities for the latitudes and longitudes listed below.

Name of City	Latitude	Longitude
1. _____	25° N	80° W
2. _____	34° N	118° W
3. _____	39° N	104° W
4. _____	42° N	71° W
5. _____	47° N	122° W

Name _____

Time Zones

Because the earth rotates on its axis, different parts of the planet face the sun at different times. People in different places see the sun rise and set at different times. Because of these time differences, the earth has been divided into twenty-four time zones. These zones begin and end at the International Date Line. Each one of them is about fifteen degrees wide. The people within each zone share a single standard time.

1. The four time zones in the continental United States are

    a. _____

    b. _____

    c. _____

    d. _____

2. The first time zone in the United States to see the sun rise in the morning is the _____

    time zone. This is true because the sun rises in the _____ and sets in the

    _____.

3. If it is 5:00 p.m. in New York City, it is _____ a.m./p.m. in Los Angeles.

4. If it is 10:00 a.m. in San Francisco, it is _____ a.m./p.m. in Miami, Florida.

Science

Ideas for Science Projects

Five False Facts

Have students pick topics from the list on page 127 and do research on these topics. Give each student twenty-six index cards. Tell students to number the cards and to record twenty true facts and five false facts about their topics, writing each fact on a separate index card. Suggest that they also record the numbers of the five false fact cards on the one remaining index card and place it in an envelope. Have each student decorate a shoe box in the theme of the study and place his or her answer and fact cards in the box. Display the boxes so that other students can read the cards and find the five false facts.

File Folder Fun

Have students pick topics from the list on page 127 for independent study. Tell them to decorate the outside of file folders to go with the topics they have chosen and to fill the inside of the folders with

- a table of contents
- five pages of information about the chosen topic
- illustrations to go with the information
- fifteen quiz questions on the information
- an answer sheet for the quiz questions
- an evaluation sheet for other students to fill out

Display folders for students to look through and learn from.

Additional Ideas

For additional project ideas, see those suggested for social studies on page 110 and adapt them as needed to science topics.

Sixty Sensational Science Topics

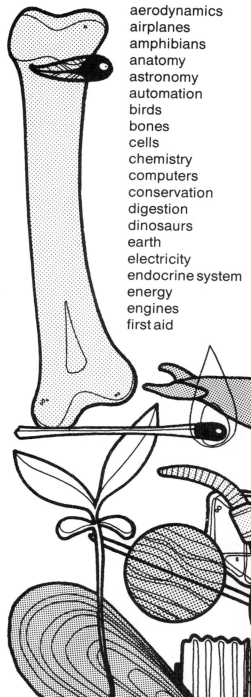

aerodynamics	fish	oceanography
airplanes	flowers	parasites
amphibians	fossils	photosynthesis
anatomy	geology	planets
astronomy	gravity	plants
automation	heart	pollution
birds	heat	prehistoric life
bones	horses	public health
cells	human body	reptiles
chemistry	insects	respiratory system
computers	inventions	rockets
conservation	invertebrates	rocks
digestion	light	senses
dinosaurs	machines	shells
earth	magnetism	solar system
electricity	mammals	sound
endocrine system	migration	tides
energy	muscular system	trees
engines	nervous system	water
first aid	nutrition	weather

Great Ideas
For Using the Lists on Pages 132-136

Pick Six Mobile

Each student selects six names from one of the lists and does research to learn about these six living things. Then the student draws, colors, and cuts out one picture of each of the six. On the back of each cutout, the student writes three to six facts about the flower, tree, fish, bird, or mammal pictured on the other side. With thread, string, or wire, the student attaches these pictures to a wire coat hanger to make a mobile. Finished mobiles can be hung in the classroom for students and visiting parents to enjoy.

Design a Stamp

Each student picks a name from one of the lists and designs a postage stamp in honor of that flower, tree, fish, bird, or mammal.

Scrambled Spelling

Each week, select five words from any one of the lists. Write these words on the board but, as you do so, scramble the letters in each one. Students will enjoy the challenge of unscrambling the letters to spell the words correctly. You may wish to add these five words to the weekly spelling list as a bonus.

Poetry Power

Each student selects a name from one of the lists and uses that plant or animal as the basis for a rhymed or unrhymed poem.

Compare and Contrast

Students select several names from one list and then quickly brainstorm among themselves to name ways in which these living things of one basic type are alike or different. For example, they might select three birds and show how their bills, feet, nests, eggs, and coloring are alike or different.

Classifying Contest

Divide students into teams of three to five. Give each team a copy of the same list. On the board write categories into which the living things on that list could be classified. For example, birds and mammals can be classified by diet (as herbivores, carnivores, insectivores, or omnivores), by activity pattern (as diurnal or nocturnal), by habitat, and by whether they are primarily predator or prey. If you are using the mammal list, you might write **diurnal** and **nocturnal** or **predator** and **prey** on the chalkboard and challenge team members to see how quickly they can correctly classify all of the mammals on the list into one of these two categories. Provide needed resources, such as dictionaries and encyclopedias, and allow time for research.

More Great Ideas
For Using the Lists on Pages 132-136

Design Time

Each student selects one topic from any of the lists on pages 132-136 and pretends that he or she has been hired by a publisher to design a dust jacket for a book on that topic. The student decides on a title, draws an appropriate illustration, and writes a summary telling what the book is about.

Create a Diorama

Each student makes a shoe box diorama showing the natural habitat of a flower, tree, fish, bird, or mammal chosen from one of the lists on pages 132-136.

Animal for a Day

Each student selects a mammal from the list on page 136. Then students pretend to be the mammals they have selected and write first-person accounts of their physical characteristics, habitats, eating habits, and daily lives.

Category Game

Rules

1. Divide the class into groups of six to eight players.

2. Reproduce enough copies of the game sheet on page 131 so that each player can have one.

3. Pick a letter of the alphabet. (Avoid the letters **Q**, **X**, **Y**, and **Z**.)

4. Name the letter and give students three minutes to write a word that begins with that letter in each of the five category boxes.

5. At the end of three minutes, students in each group compare answers. If two students in a group have the same answer, both of them must cross off that answer and receive no points for it.

6. Students record their scores for each round. They receive one point for each answer that is both correct and unique within the group.

7. Pick another letter and play a second round in the same manner.

8. After five rounds, total the individual round scores. Add a bonus point for each column in which there are no blanks, incorrect answers, or words that have been crossed off because of duplication.

9. At the end of five rounds, the student in each group with the highest score is declared the winner for that group.

Example

Round	Letter	**Flower**	**Tree**	**Fish**	**Bird**	**Mammal**	Score
1	S	sunflower	spruce	snapper	swallow	sheep	5
2	D	daisy	dogwood		dove	dog	4
3	R	rose			raven	rat	3
4	P	petunia	pine	perch	pelican	~~porcupine~~	4
5	A	aster	ash			anteater	3

Total	19
Bonus	1
Final Score	20

Name _____

Category Game Sheet

Round	Letter	Flower	Tree	Fish	Bird	Mammal	Score
1							
2							
3							
4							
5							

Total

Bonus

Final Score

Flower Power

anemone
apple blossom
aster
azalea
begonia
black-eyed susan
bluebell
buttercup
camellia
carnation
chrysanthemum
coneflower
cowslip
crocus
daffodil
daisy
dandelion
dogwood
edelweiss
forget-me-not
forsythia
foxglove
freesia
fuchsia
gardenia
geranium
gladiolus
goldenrod
heather
hibiscus
hollyhock

hyacinth
hydrangea
iris
jasmine
jonquil
lady's slipper
lantana
larkspur
lilac
lily of the valley
marigold
narcissus
nasturtium
orchid
pansy
peach blossom
peony
petunia
poppy
ranunculus
rhododendron
rose
snapdragon
sunflower
sweet pea
thistle
tulip
violet
wisteria
yucca
zinnia

Treasury of Trees

ailanthus
alder
almond
apple
ash
aspen
beech
birch
cedar
cherry
chestnut
cycad
cypress
deodar
elm
eucalyptus
fig
fir
grapefruit
hazel
hemlock
hickory
larch
lemon
lime
linden
locust
magnolia
mahogany
maple
myrtle
oak
olive
orange
palm
palmetto
peach
pear
pecan
pine
poplar
sequoia
spruce
sycamore
walnut
willow
yew

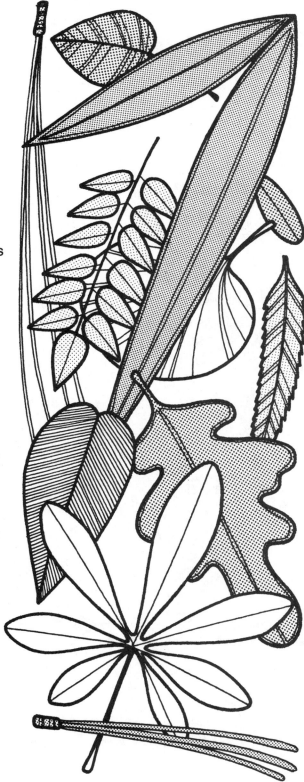

Fish Frenzy

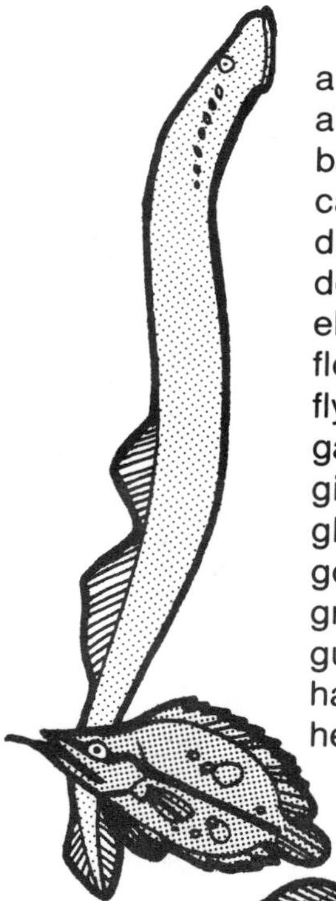

anemone fish
angelfish
barracuda
carp
discus
dolphin
electric eel
flounder
flying fish
garfish
giant sea bass
glass catfish
goldfish
grunion
guppy
haddock
head-and-tail-light

herring
lamprey eel
leaf fish
lionfish
mackerel
mollienisia
Moorish idol
moray eel
mudskipper
neon tetra
paddlefish
perch
pike
pipefish
piranha
puffer
sailfish

salmon
sargassum fish
sawfish
sea horse
Siamese fighting fish
skate
stickleback
stingray
sturgeon
sunfish
swordfish
triggerfish
trout
trunkfish
tuna
white shark
wrasse

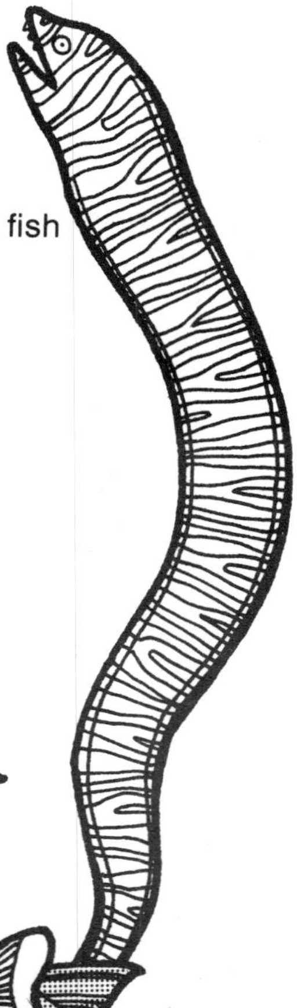

Bunches of Birds

albatross
anhinga
auk
avocet
bird of paradise
bittern
bluebird
bobolink
bobwhite
booby
bowerbird
cardinal
cassowary
cedar waxwing
chickadee
chicken
cockatoo
cock of the rock
condor
cormorant
crow
cuckoo
dipper
dodo
dove
duck
eagle
egret
emu
falcon
flamingo
flicker
flycatcher

frogmouth
goldfinch
goose
grebe
guinea fowl
gull
hawk
heron
honey guide
hornbill
hummingbird
ibis
jackdaw
jay
kestrel
kingfisher
kiwi
kookaburra
loon
lorikeet
lovebird
lyrebird
macaw
magpie
meadowlark
mockingbird
myna
nuthatch
oriole
osprey
ostrich
ovenbird
owl

oyster catcher
parakeet
parrot
peafowl
pelican
penguin
pheasant
pigeon
puffin
quail
quetzal
raven
rhea
roadrunner
robin
secretary bird
spoonbill
starling
stork
sunbird
swallow
swan
swift
tanager
tern
toucan
touraco
turkey
vulture
warbler
whydah
woodpecker
wren

Mammal Mania

aardvark	giraffe	ocelot
addax	gnu	okapi
anteater	gopher	opossum
armadillo	gorilla	orangutan
aye-aye	hamster	otter
baboon	hartebeest	panda
badger	hedgehog	pangolin
bat	hippopotamus	peccary
bear	horse	platypus
beaver	hyena	porcupine
bison	hyrax	prairie dog
camel	ibex	rabbit
capybara	jackal	raccoon
caracal	jaguar	rhinoceros
cat (domestic)	kangaroo	seal
chamois	kinkajou	shrew
cheetah	klipspringer	skunk
chimpanzee	koala	sloth
chinchilla	lemming	squirrel
chipmunk	lemur	tapir
civet	leopard	thylacine
coati	lion	tiger
coyote	llama	walrus
deer	lynx	warthog
dik-dik	manatee	weasel
dog (domestic)	markhor	whale
eland	marmoset	wolf
elephant	mink	wolverine
fox	mole	wombat
galago	mongoose	woodchuck
gerbil	moose	yak
gerenuk	mouse	zebra
gibbon	musk-ox	zebu

Name _____

Science Project Worksheet

Topic, Title, and Type

Topic: _____

Title: _____

Type: ☐ biological science   ☐ physical science

Hypothesis

I think that if I _____

_____

_____

_____ ,

then _____

_____

_____ .

Materials and Equipment

_____   _____

_____   _____

_____   _____

_____   _____

_____   _____

Procedure

_____

_____

_____

_____

_____

Results

_____

_____

_____

Conclusions

_____

_____

_____

Computer Talk

BASIC
Beginning All-Purpose Symbolic Instruction Code, the computer language designed for education but now used by business

binary system
a system in which the digits 0 and 1 are used and numbers are grouped by powers of two

bit
a storage cell in a computer's memory

byte
a group of bits

cartridge
box or case that contains a cassette tape

central processing unit (CPU)
the integrated circuits that form the processing and memory units of a computer

character
any letter, digit, punctuation mark, or symbol that a programmer uses when processing data

chip
thumbnail-sized integrated electrical circuit used to build the processing and memory units of today's computers

circuit
the path of an electric current

COBOL
Common Business Oriented Language, the computer language used mainly in business

code
a group of lines, letters, or symbols that can be read and understood by a computer

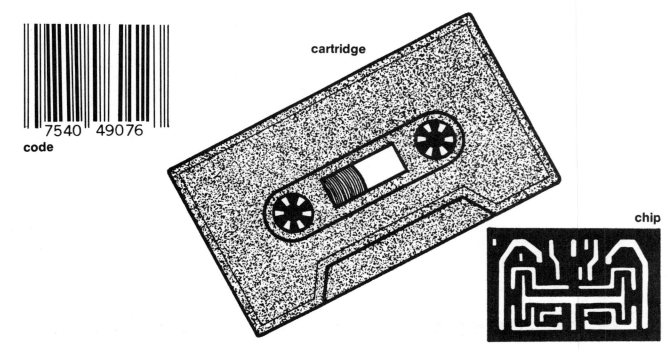

7540 49076
code

cartridge

chip

More Computer Talk

computer   a programmable electronic machine that works with numbers

cursor   a lighted or blinking shape on the video screen which marks the spot where a message will be printed or a symbol or color will appear if a key on the keyboard is pressed

data   numbers and information that are given to a computer

erase   to rub out, get rid of, or do away with

floppy disc   a disc that looks like a 45-rpm record on which programs can be stored

flow chart   a graphic outline of the steps that are necessary to do a specific job

FORTRAN   Formula Translation, the computer language used mainly by mathematicians, scientists, and engineers

graphics   pictures and colors that can be programmed to appear on a computer's video screen

flow chart

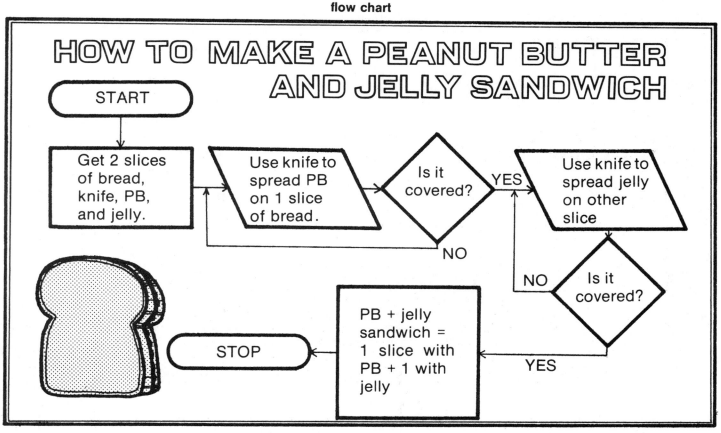

More Computer Talk

hardware   the working mechanical and electrical parts of a computer, including the video screen, central processing unit, keyboard, disc drive, and printer

input   operating step during which information is put into, or given to, a computer; the information that is put into a computer

computer hardware

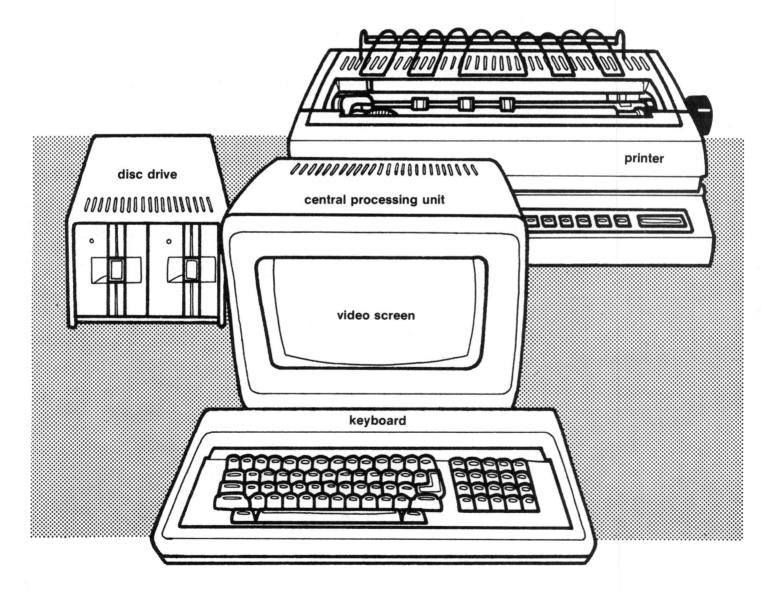

printer

disc drive

central processing unit

video screen

keyboard

More Computer Talk

keyboard   the piece of computer hardware that looks like a typewriter and is used to give information to the computer

memory   operating step during which the computer stores or recalls data or orders it has been given; the part of the central processing unit in which data are stored; the capacity of the computer to store data

output   operating step during which the computer presents its answer, response, or results in usable form; the answer, response, or results presented by the computer

printer   the piece of computer hardware that types printed output, or printout

printout   computer output that is typed, or printed out, on paper

processing   the operating step during which the computer rearranges data, tests them, and uses them to work math problems

program   a series or set of instructions given to a computer in a language it can understand

programmer   a person who knows at least one computer language and uses it to give instructions to a computer

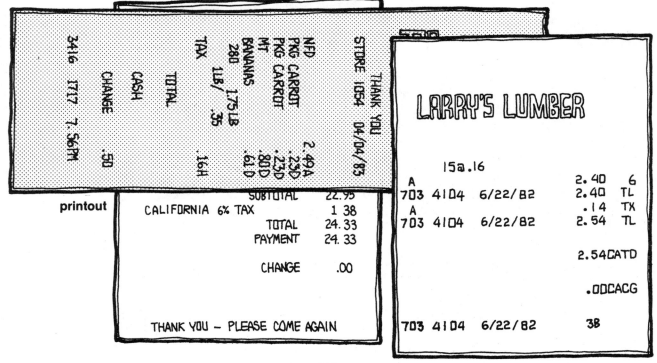

printout

The Teacher's Pet
© 1983 — The Learning Works, Inc.

More Computer Talk

software any program used on a computer, which may be stored on punched cards, floppy discs, cassette tapes, or reels of tape

transistor a tiny electronic device that acts like a switch and controls the flow of electric current in a chip

video game a game made up of action choices programmed on a tape or disc and played with graphics on a video screen

video screen the piece of computer hardware that looks like a television set and displays symbols, words, numbers, or colors

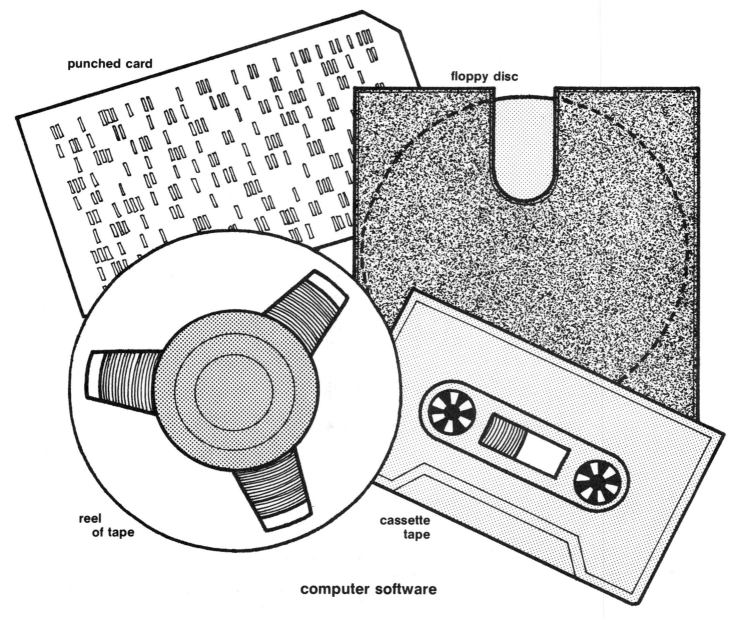

punched card

floppy disc

reel of tape

cassette tape

computer software

Hobbies and Occupations

Field	Person	Subject of Study or Interest
agronomy	agronomist	soil
anthropology	anthropologist	man
archaeology	archaeologist	ancient civilizations
astronomy	astronomer	celestial bodies
audiology	audiologist	hearing
biology	biologist	living organisms
cardiology	cardiologist	heart
conchology	conchologist	shells
criminology	criminologist	crime
dermatology	dermatologist	skin
endocrinology	endocrinologist	glands
entomology	entomologist	insects
genealogy	genealogist	families and ancestors
geology	geologist	rocks
geophysics	geophysicist	earth
graphology	graphologist	handwriting
helminthology	helminthologist	parasitic worms
hematology	hematologist	blood and blood-forming organs
herpetology	herpetologist	amphibians and reptiles

Hobbies and Occupations
(continued)

Field	Person	Subject of Study or Interest
horticulture	horticulturist	fruits, vegetables, flowers, or ornamental plants
hydrology	hydrologist	water
ichthyology	ichthyologist	fish
malacology	malacologist	mollusks
mammalogy	mammalologist	mammals
numerology	numerologist	numbers
numismatics	numismatist	coins, tokens, medals, and paper money
ophthalmology	ophthalmologist	eye
ornithology	ornithologist	birds
osteology	osteologist	bones
otology	otologist	ear
paleontology	paleontologist	fossils
pathology	pathologist	diseased tissues
philately	philatelist	stamps
philology	philologist	literature or linguistics
phrenology	phrenologist	skulls
podiatry	podiatrist	feet
psychology	psychologist	mind; mental processes and activities
zoology	zoologist	animals

Awards

All-Purpose Awards

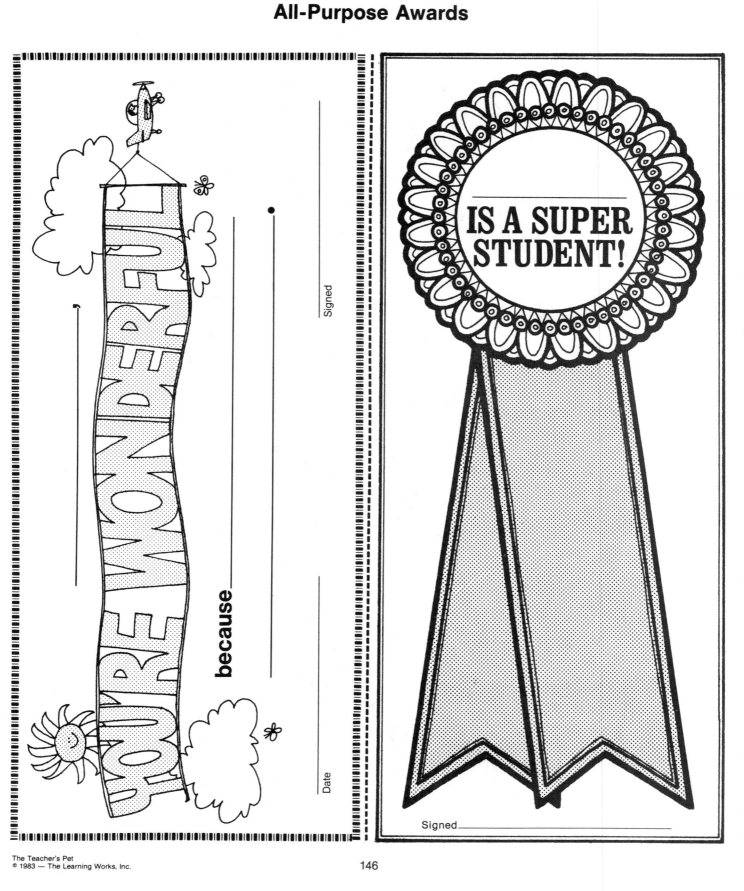

YOU'RE WONDERFUL

because

Signed

Date

IS A SUPER STUDENT!

Signed

Effort and Improvement Awards

ENORMOUS EFFORT AWARD

EARNED BY _____

FOR _____ .

Date _____   Signed _____

INTRODUCING NEW, IMPROVED

_____ !

YOU'RE GETTING BETTER

Date _____   Signed _____

Reading and Book Reporting Awards

BRILLIANT BOOK REPORT AWARD

PRESENTED TO

_____

FOR AN OUTSTANDING REPORT ON

_____ .

Signed _____

Date _____

FOR READING _____ BOOKS, _____

HAS BEEN OFFICIALLY DECLARED A

BOOKWORM.

Date _____

Signed _____

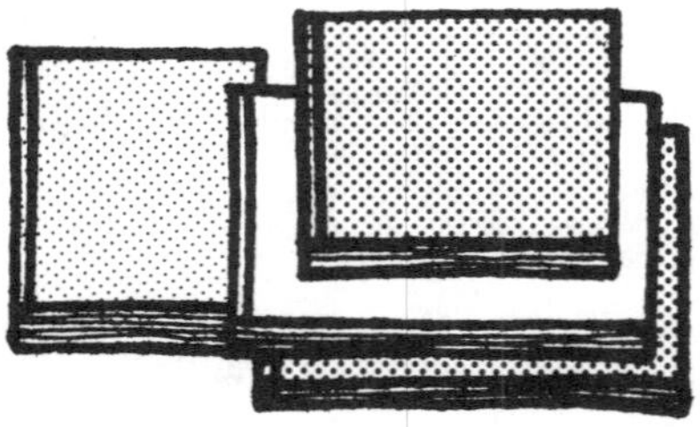

Spelling and Handwriting Awards

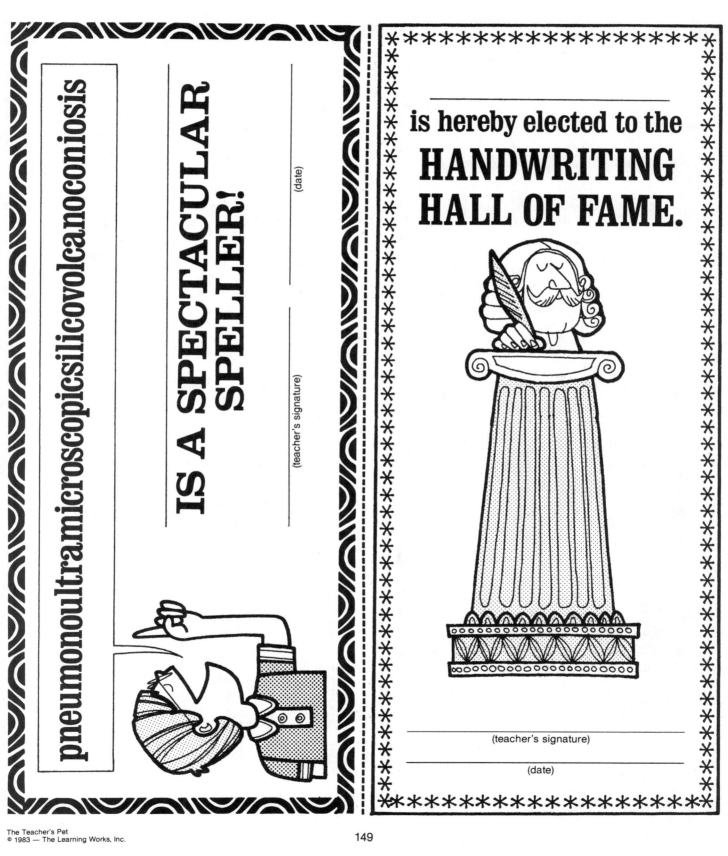

pneumonoultramicroscopicsilicovolcanoconiosis

IS A SPECTACULAR SPELLER!

(teacher's signature)

(date)

_____
is hereby elected to the

HANDWRITING HALL OF FAME.

(teacher's signature)

(date)

Other Language Arts Awards

Be it hereby declared and made known to all who enjoy good stories that _____ wrote

A WHALE OF A TALE.

_____
(teacher's signature)

_____
(date)

GIVEN TO

_____

IN RECOGNITION OF WORD WIZARDRY

_____
(teacher's signature)

_____
(date)

Addition and Subtraction Awards

4367054 76085
+2308284 32590
6675339 08675

_____ IS A

FANTASTIC ADDER!

_____   _____
(teacher's signature)   (date)

MINUS MAN
SAYS THAT

_____
IS A SUPER
SUBTRACTER.

_____
(date)

35684384027

Multiplication and Division Awards

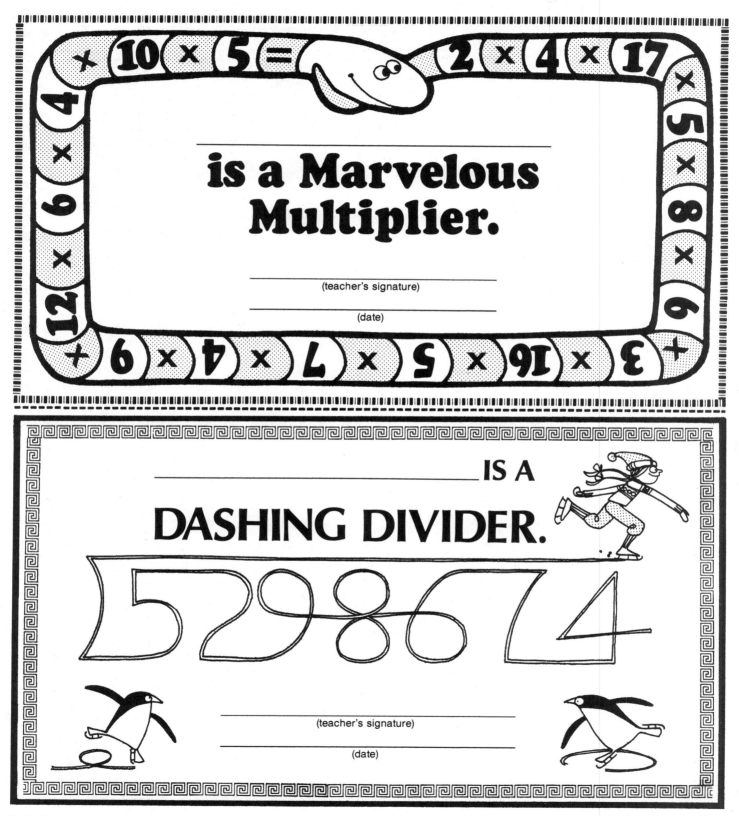

_____

is a Marvelous Multiplier.

_____
(teacher's signature)

_____
(date)

_____ IS A

DASHING DIVIDER.

_____
(teacher's signature)

_____
(date)

Other Math Awards

IN RECOGNITION OF ABSOLUTELY ASTOUNDING FEATS PERFORMED WITH NUMBERS,

_____

HAS BEEN NAMED A
MATH MAGICIAN.

Signature
Date

AWARDED TO

_____

FOR MASTERING THE
MATH
MONSTER

Signature _____

Date _____

Social Studies Awards

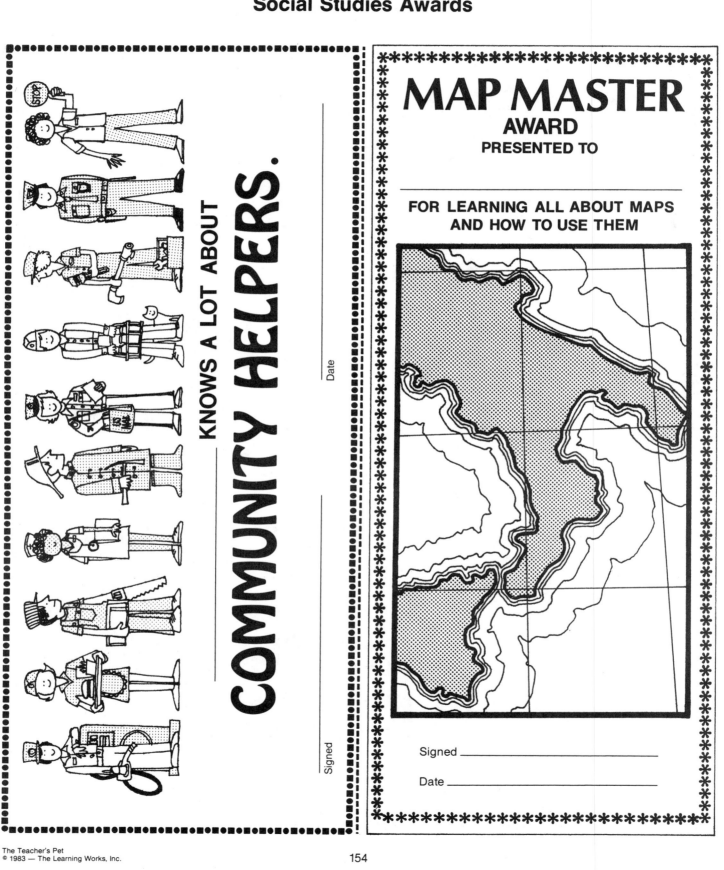

KNOWS A LOT ABOUT

COMMUNITY HELPERS.

Signed

Date

MAP MASTER
AWARD
PRESENTED TO

FOR LEARNING ALL ABOUT MAPS
AND HOW TO USE THEM

Signed _____

Date _____

Science Awards

After extensive investigation,

_____

has proved to be a

SUPER
SCIENCE SLEUTh.

Signature _____

Date _____

SUPER SCIENTIST CERTIFICATE

Awarded to _____

in recognition of curiosity and discovery

_____
Date

_____
Signed

Art and Sports Awards

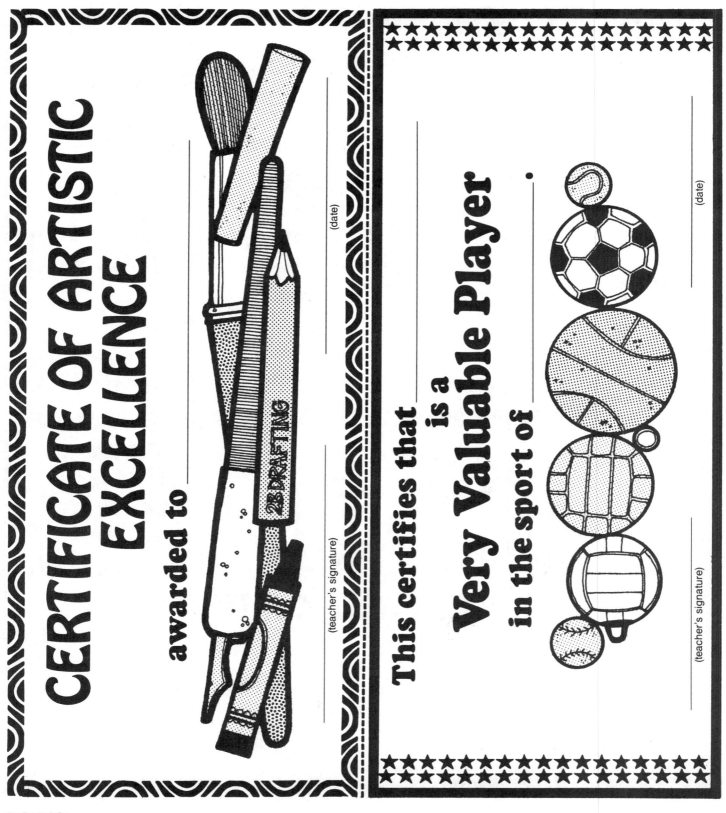

CERTIFICATE OF ARTISTIC EXCELLENCE

awarded to

_____

(date)

(teacher's signature)

This certifies that

_____

is a

Very Valuable Player

in the sport of _____

(date)

(teacher's signature)

Holiday Happenings

Name _____

Back-to-School Apples

The ready-to-use art on pages 158-169 is ideal for individualizing instruction and is easy to turn into custom-made activity sheets to present, review, or reinforce a skill at any grade or interest level. Fill these pages with math problems or with spelling and vocabulary words. Encourage students to create their own problems or to use these pages as game boards or game cards. Add row or column letters, and turn them into bingo-style find, match, and cover games. Put these pages to work in reading readiness practice, following directions activities, and art projects or in other creative ways.

Name _____

Floating Ghosts

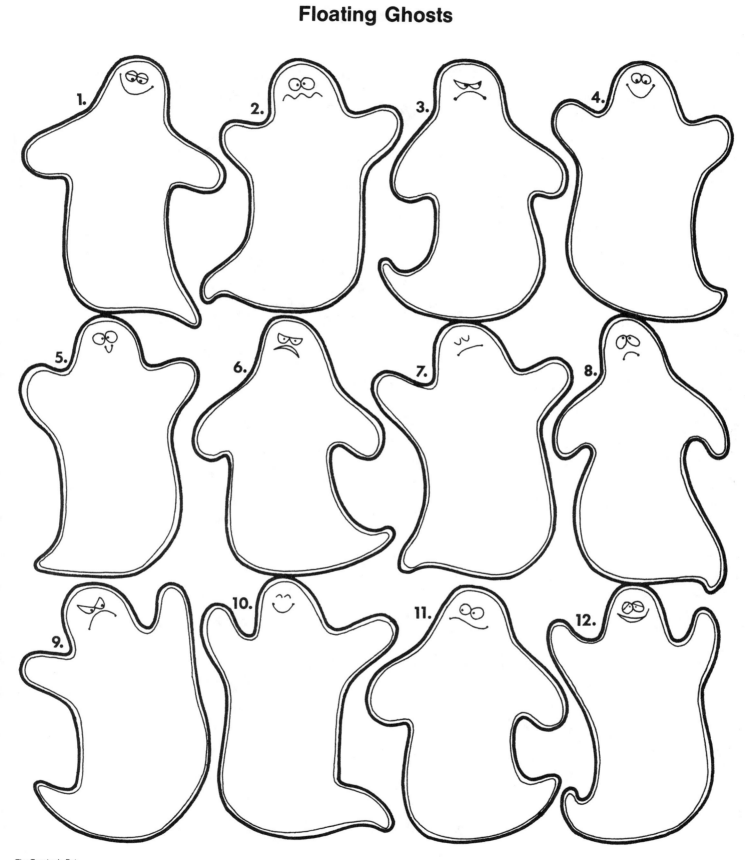

Name _____

Turkey Trot

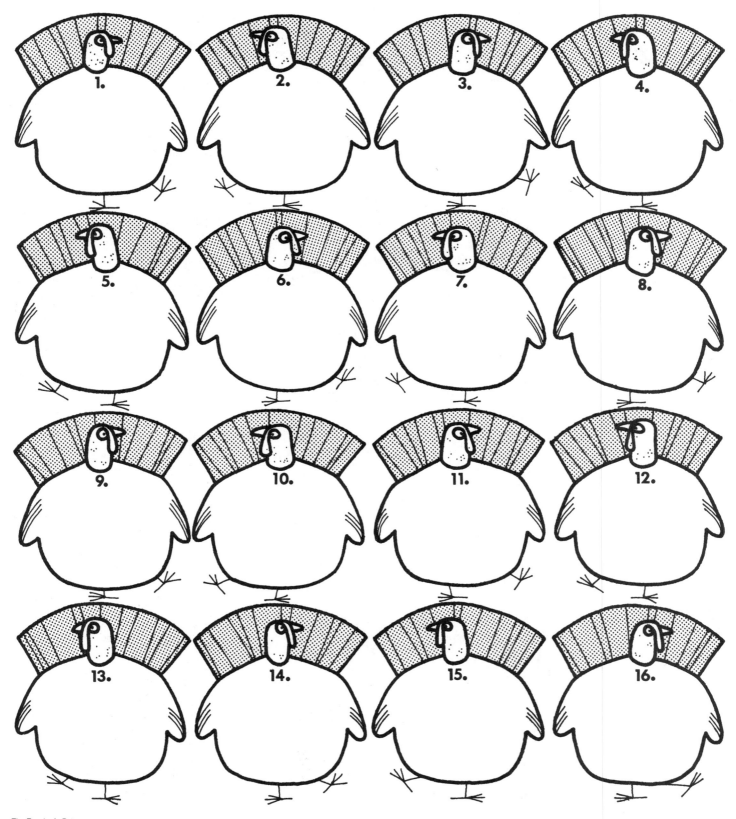

Pick a Package

Name _____

Happy New Year Hats

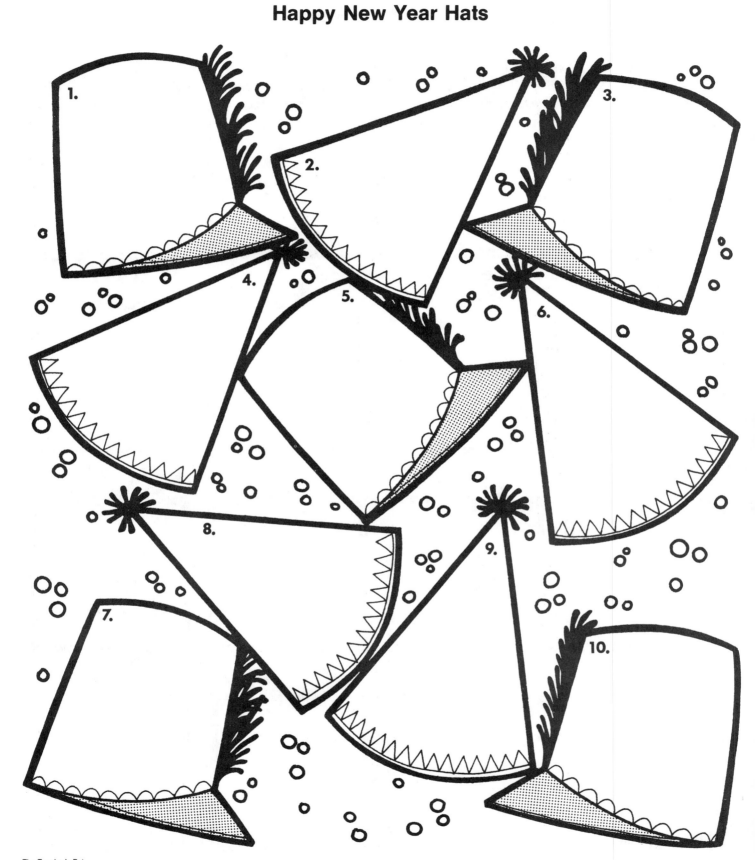

Name _____

Have a Heart

Name _____

Lucky Shamrocks

Name _____

Funny Bunnies

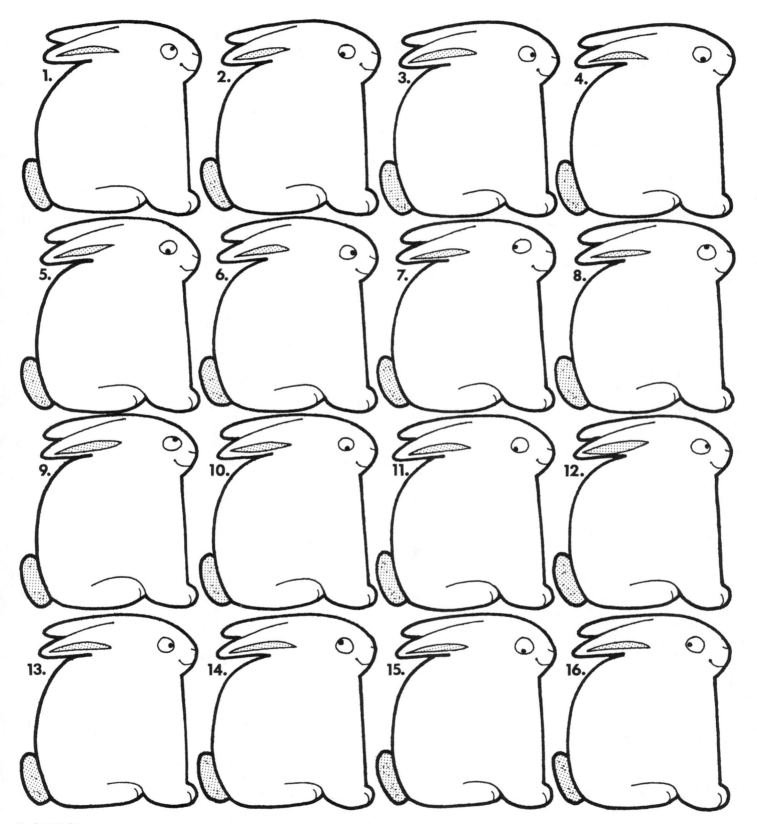

Name _____

Kite Flight

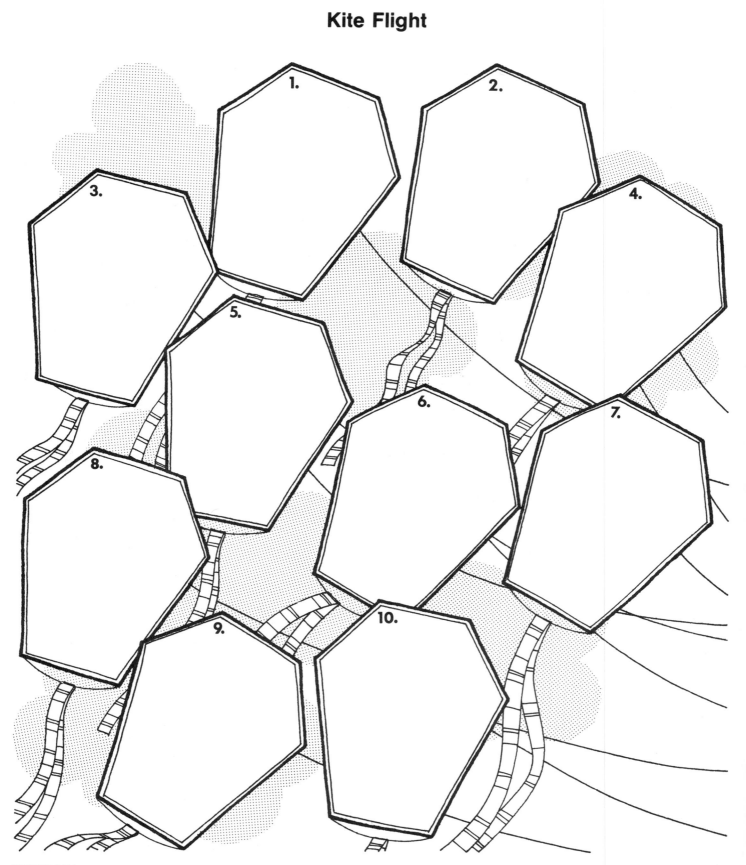

Name _____

Summer Suns

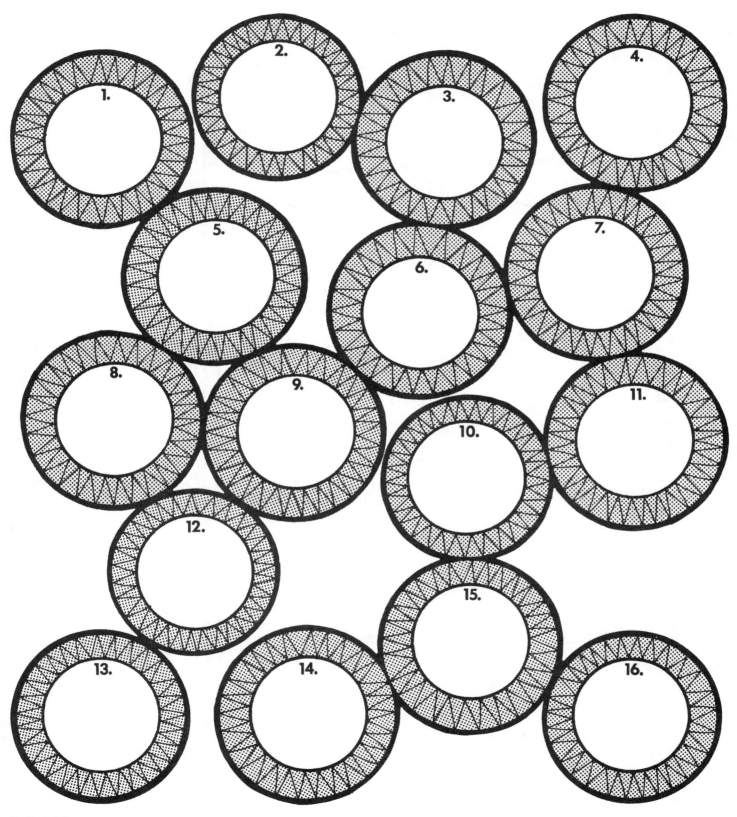

Name _____

Flying Flags

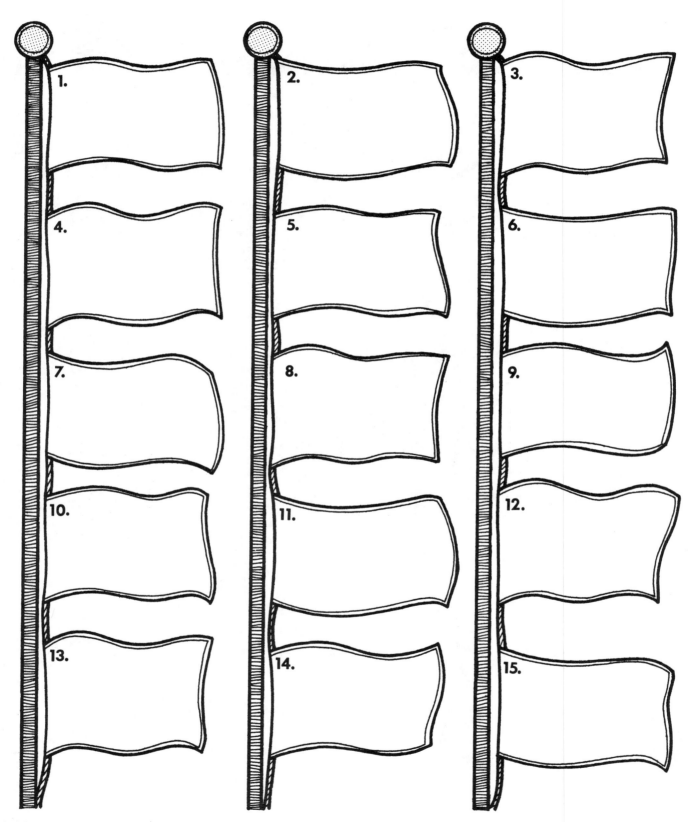

Name _____

Dandy Daisies

Clip Art

On this page and pages 171-181 are theme-related drawings that you can use to create your own activity cards, announcements, awards, contracts, flyers, game boards, invitations, name tags, and programs, and to add a touch of whimsy to worksheets and tests. These drawings are grouped by subject or theme. Specific themes include animals, characters and careers, discoveries and inventions, holidays, space exploration, sports, and transportation. One page, entitled On Stage, is devoted entirely to pictures that are especially appropriate for use on programs for class or school concerts, pageants, and plays.

Although this art is theme-related, it is readily adaptable to any classroom occasion or school year event. All you need to do is duplicate the page (so you can use the clip art on the other side later), clip out the drawing you wish to use, attach it to the sheet you intend to decorate, and reproduce the sheet with art in place.

With the help of an opaque projector or squared paper, you can enlarge clip art drawings for other applications. For example, you can make them large enough for effective use on bulletin boards, posters, and signs. You can also use them as patterns for book covers, borders, greeting cards, and other student- or teacher-made art.

Happy Holidays

Happy Holidays
(continued)

Happy Holidays
(continued)

Ways to Go

Space Race

Sports Shorts

Discoveries and Inventions

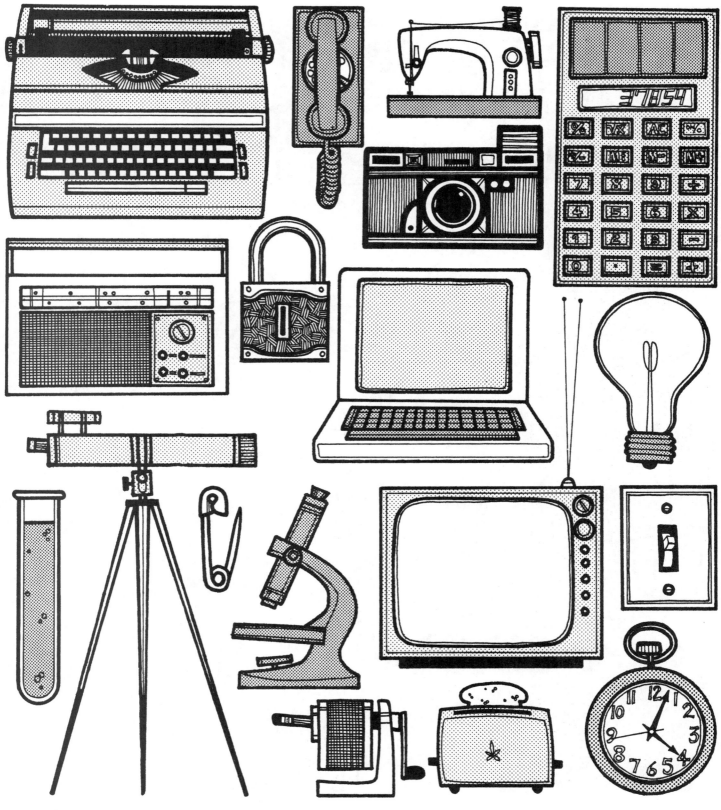

Animal Antics

On Stage

Characters and Careers

Characters and Careers
(continued)

Borders

Borders cover rough edges, make any display look more finished, and add a seasonal or holiday touch to subject matter bulletin boards. They can easily be cut paper-doll style from folded lengths of paper or fabric.

Colored construction paper is probably the most widely used border material; however, for interesting effects, try felt, foil, gift wrap, newspaper, patterned shelf paper, plaid or print fabric, or wallpaper. For variety, combine and overlap borders of different but compatible shapes or borders of the same shape cut from paper or fabric of different shades or colors.

To create a border, first decide whether you intend to run bands across the top and bottom, down the sides, or entirely around your board. Measure this distance in inches. Divide the total distance in inches by the length of a single strip, also in inches, to determine how many strips of paper or fabric you need. Cut that number of strips.

Fold each strip in half and then in half again. Photocopy or trace any of the patterns on pages 183–191. Position the pattern on your folded paper or fabric as shown, draw around it with a pencil or chalk, and cut out the resulting shape. Carefully unfold the strip.

The borders on the following pages have been designed to make efficient use of a 12-inch-by-18-inch piece of construction paper. Most of them can be cut from either a folded 12-inch strip or a folded 18-inch strip. Note the dimensions given beside each pattern.

Acorns and Leaves

Acorns

Cut from 3-inch-by-18-inch strips folded to be 3-inch-by-4½-inch rectangles. For best results, place the stem edge on the thick fold. Vary by using a felt-tipped pen to darken the caps and stems or by cutting them from paper of a darker shade and gluing or stapling them to the border.

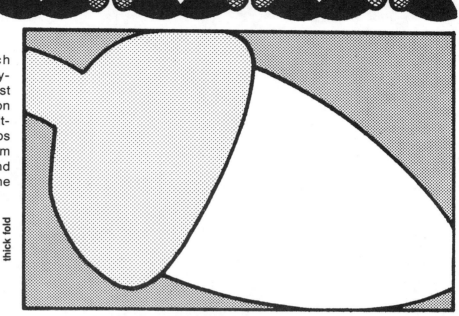

thick fold

Grape Leaves

Cut from 4-inch-by-18-inch strips folded to be 4-inch-by-4½-inch rectangles. For best results, place the stem edge on the thick fold. Vary by using red, orange, yellow, and brown paper and mixing or overlapping strips of different colors. For spring, use shades of green.

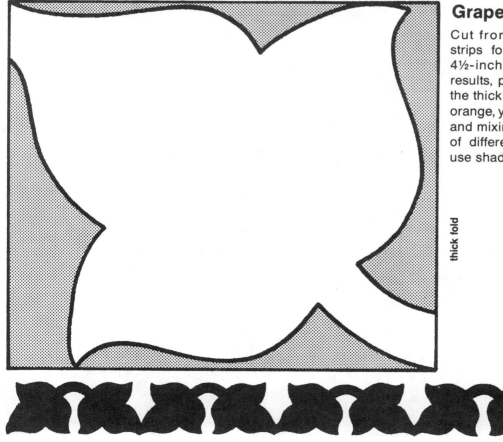

thick fold

Pumpkins and Cats

Pumpkins

Cut from 4-inch-by-18-inch strips folded to be 4-inch-by-4½-inch rectangles. For variety, separately cut brown or green stems and glue them over the existing ones. Just for fun, use a black felt-tipped marking pen to transform some or all of the pumpkins into jack-o'-lanterns. Follow the pattern suggested here or create your own.

Black Cats

These cats won't bring bad luck if you pin, staple, or tack them securely to a bulletin board or wall. Cut them from 4-inch-by-18-inch strips folded to be 4-inch-by-4½-inch rectangles.

Ships and Turkeys

Ships

Ships under sail are reminiscent of the early explorers and settlers. Cut them from 4-inch-by-12-inch strips folded to be 4-inch-by-3-inch rectangles.

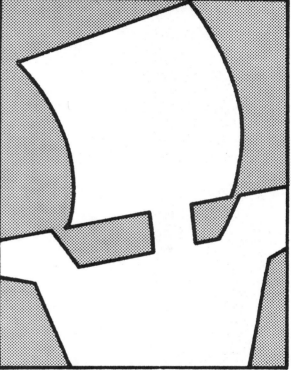

Turkeys

Thanksgiving wouldn't be complete without a turkey. Here's a whole flock of them to band or border your bulletin boards. Cut them from 3-inch-by-18-inch strips folded to be 3-inch-by-4½-inch rectangles.

Mice and Bells

Mice

For a December display, mice are nice. Cut them from 4-inch-by-12-inch strips folded to be 4-inch-by-3-inch rectangles. For best results, place the mouse's feet on the thick fold. Just for fun, use a felt-tipped marking pen to draw eyes and whiskers on some or all of your mice. Then glue on noses and ear linings cut from pink paper or felt. Follow the pattern provided here or create your own.

thick fold

Bells

Bells ring out the old year and ring in the new. Cut them from 3-inch-by-12-inch strips folded to be 3-inch-by-3-inch squares. For best results, place the top edge of the bell on the thick fold.

thick fold

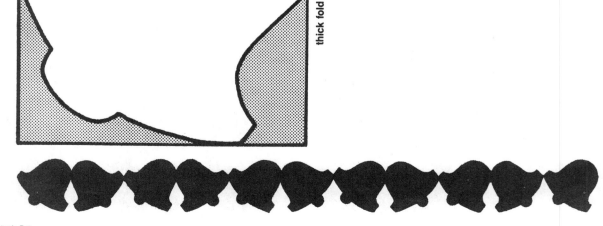

Snowmen and Mittens

Snowmen

Welcome winter with a row of men made of snow. Cut them from 4½-inch-by-12-inch strips folded to be 4½-inch-by-3-inch rectangles. Just for fun, use a black felt-tipped marking pen to give some or all of your snowmen a black top hat, black eyes, a button nose, and a friendly smile.

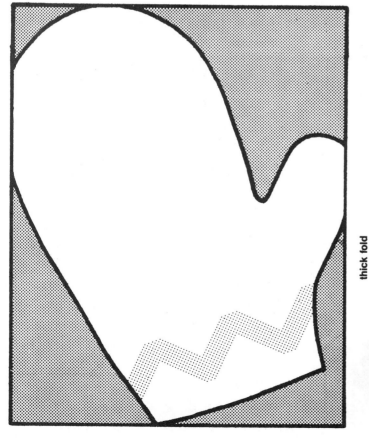

thick fold

Mittens

Keep out the winter cold with colorful mittens—not just a pair but a whole band or border of them. Cut them from 4½-inch-by-14-inch strips folded to be 4½-inch-by-3½-inch rectangles. For best results, position the pattern so that the thumb is at the thick fold. Just for fun, decorate the mittens with zigzags or other simple designs drawn or cut from paper of contrasting colors.

Hats and Hearts

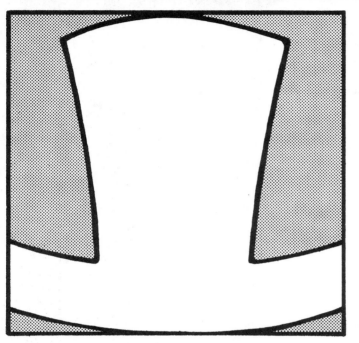

Horizontal Hats

Commemorate Abraham Lincoln's birthday with a row of top hats. Cut them from 3½-inch-by-14-inch strips folded to be 3½-inch-by-3½-inch squares.

Vertical Hearts

Greet February with a bright border of hearts. Cut them from 4½-inch-by-16-inch strips folded to be 4½-inch-by-4-inch rectangles. For best results, place the top of the heart on the thick fold.

thick fold

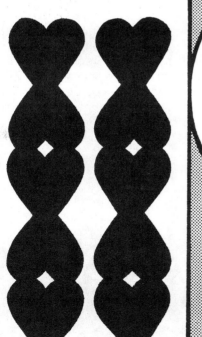

Shamrocks and Tulips

Shamrocks

Sure an' begorra, St. Patrick's Day is the time to wish for the luck o' the Irish and to wear a little green. Cut these shamrocks from 4-inch-by-18-inch strips folded to be 4-inch-by-4½-inch rectangles.

Tulips

March 20 or 21 is the Vernal Equinox, the first day of spring. Welcome this season with a border of pink, yellow, or red tulips. Cut them from 4-inch-by-18-inch strips folded to be 4-inch-by-4½-inch rectangles.

Umbrellas and Bunnies

Umbrellas

When April showers dampen your day, lift spirits with bands or borders of bright umbrellas. Cut them from 4-inch-by-16-inch strips folded to be 4-inch-by-4-inch squares.

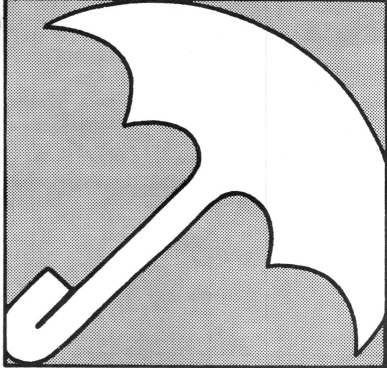

Bunches of Bunnies

For Easter or for spring, border a bulletin board with a bunch of bunnies. Cut them from 4½-inch-by-12-inch strips folded to be 4½-inch-by-3-inch rectangles. For variety, cut bunnies from paper in pastel colors rather than from white. Just for fun, use a felt-tipped marking pen to draw facial features on some or all of your bunnies. Follow the pattern provided here or create your own.

Daisies and Suns

Daisies

April showers bring May flowers. Freshen your room with dozens of daisies. Cut them from 4-inch-by-8-inch white strips folded to be 4-inch-by-2-inch rectangles. For best results, place the daisy center on the thick fold. After cutting, carefully unfold each 2-daisy strip. As a variation, use a crayon or felt-tipped marking pen to add yellow centers or cut them from yellow construction paper and glue them in place.

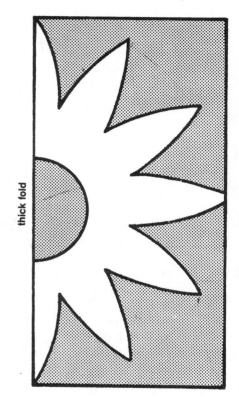

Suns

When May comes, the hot summer sun is not many days away. Cut these suns from yellow or orange 4-inch-by-16-inch strips folded to be 4-inch-by-4-inch squares and then folded once more to yield 4-inch-by-2-inch-rectangles. For best results, place the center of the sun on the thick fold. As a variation, cut daisy shapes from orange paper and then pin, tack, staple, or glue them on yellow suns.

Answer Key

Page 90, Pickled Plurals
1. heroes 2. spoonfuls *or* spoonsful 3. mothers-in-law
4. elves 5. ibex *or* ibexes 6. sheep 7. glasses 8. vertexes
or vertices 9. biographies 10. volcanoes *or* volcanos
11. routines 12. bacteria 13. beaches 14. fungi 15. octo-
puses *or* octopi 16. women 17. turkeys 18. foxes
19. vertebrae *or* vertebras 20. amoebas *or* amoebae

Page 92, Spelling Riddle
Question: Where does a lamb go when it needs a
haircut?
Answer: To the baa baa shop.

Page 93, What Would You Do With . . . ?
Eat It: ambrosia, aspic, escargot, jicama, papaya,
pumpernickel, tofu, vichyssoise
Wear It: beret, monocle, peplum, snood, tiara, tippet,
toga, tutu
Play It: calliope, celesta, fife, ocarina, spinet, timbrel,
tympani, zither

Page 96, The Case of the Missing Masterpiece
The thief was Samantha Strand, who left the museum at
5:20.

Page 102, The Sum's the Same

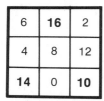

6	**16**	2
4	8	12
14	0	**10**

1. The sum is **24**.

9	19	5
7	**11**	**15**
17	3	13

2. The sum is 33.

10	**20**	6
8	**12**	16
18	4	**14**

3. The sum is 36.

7	17	3
5	**9**	13
15	1	11

4. The sum is **27**.

Page 103, How Strong Is Your Addition?

	a	b	c	d	e
1	11	17	20	19	12
2	37	61	144	119	142
3	542	447	904	323	763
4	164	222	150	252	151
5	977	1,295	1,587	1,381	1,238

Page 104, Find Five Subtraction Quiz
1d 2c 3e 4e 5d

Page 105, Multiplication Quiz

	a	b	c	d	e
1	42	64	63	30	56
2	52	208	306	522	441
3	486	1,760	1,040	3,285	4,617
4	2,968	15,600	35,757	48,564	54,870
5	26,668	468,356	385,578	263,172	345,664

Page 106, Doughnuts Division

	a	b	c	d	e
1	13	26	34	58	63
2	27	55	40	45	81
3	19r7	2r28	14r11	6r15	6r5
4	28r28	5r55	11r143	7r383	6r495

Page 108, More Graphs Galore
Bar Graph: 1. dogs 2. snakes 3. hamsters 4. 11
Picture Graph: 1. three million 2. Australia 3. Peru, Iraq,
and Uruguay 4. three million
Line Graph: 1. August 2. February 3. 9 tons 4. October
Circle Graph: 1. soccer 2. tennis 3. jogging 4. jogging
and soccer

Page 113, Map Quiz
1. Rhode Island 2. Alaska, Texas, California 3. Kan-
sas 4. Montana 5. Oregon, Nevada, Arizona 6. Wisconsin
7. Maine 8. California 9. Nevada, Oregon, Washington,
Montana, Wyoming, and Utah 10. Texas 11. Hawaii
12. Kentucky

Page 123, Latitude and Longitude
1. Miami, Florida 2. Los Angeles, California 3. Denver,
Colorado 4. Boston, Massachusetts 5. Seattle, Washington

Page 124, Time Zones
1. a. Eastern b. Central c. Mountain d. Pacific
2. Eastern, east, west 3. 2:00 p.m. 4. 1:00 p.m.